D1459937

Simple
CROCHET

Creative Makers

Simple
CROCHET

With more than 35 vintage-vibe projects for your handmade life

SARA SINAGUGLIA

PHOTOGRAPHY BY YUKI SUGIURA • DESIGNED BY ANITA MANGAN

Mitchell Beazley

Simple Crochet by Sara Sinaguglia

First published in Great Britain in 2012
by Mitchell Beazley, an imprint of Octopus
Publishing Group Ltd, Endeavour House,
189 Shaftesbury Avenue, London,
WC2H 8JY
www.octopusbooksusa.com

An Hachette UK Company
www.hachette.co.uk

This edition published in 2013

Distributed in the US by
Hachette Book Group USA
237 Park Avenue
New York NY 10017 USA

Distributed in Canada by
Canadian Manda Group
165 Dufferin Street
Toronto, Ontario, Canada M6K 3H6

ISBN 978-1-84533-834-3

Set in Berthold Akzidenz Grotesk and Bulmer

Printed and bound in China

Publisher: Alison Starling
Managing Editor: Clare Churly
Assistant Editor: Stephanie Milner
Copyeditor: Eleanor Van Zandt
Pattern Checker: Susan Horan
Senior Art Editor: Juliette Norsworthy
Designer: Anita Mangan
Design Assistant: Abi Read
Photographer: Yuki Sugiura
Stylist: Cynthia Inions
Senior Production Controller: Caroline Alberti

CONTENTS

INTRODUCTION

Crochet is a simple craft that offers endless opportunities for creativity to flourish. With just a hook and some yarn, you can relax and simply switch off. It's much less demanding, for me, than knitting.

I grew up with the familiar sound of my Grandma Connie's knitting needles clack-clacking away of an evening. Connie was a prolific knitter, and she taught me to knit when I was about eight years old (she also taught me to play a mean hand of cards). I have carried this skill throughout my life, but I am an absent-minded knitter, easily distracted by other things, incapable of counting my stitches and frustrated by following patterns.

It was when my husband Giuseppe (also known as The Sicilian), and I moved to our little cottage in the Dorset countryside that I rediscovered yarn. Taking pity on our shivering from the drafty windows and chilly winters, Mom offered me the crocheted granny square blankets that Connie had made for my brother and me when we were small. With them came wonderful memories of hot stone water bottles nestled at the bottom of our freezing beds, cuddles, stories, and much, much more. However, my own children, Sofia (fondly referred to as Pipi) and Dante, weren't quite so enamored of these acrylic grannies adorning their beds. It wasn't just

the mismatched colors; they had grown up spoilt by my mom's beautiful soft wool and cotton hand-knits, and acrylic just doesn't have the same snuggle factor.

Realizing that the entire cottage needed "cozying up" a bit, I set about learning to crochet. Under the expert and patient guidance of my friend Lena, I fumbled my way around a three-sided granny "square" (it was meant to be four-sided but I kept forgetting to turn the corner). Inspired by Lena's projects, I refused to let this little motif get the better of me, so on I labored. And before long, it all slipped into place. The real joy came from never having to deal with more than one stitch on my hook at any given time (unlike those problematical rows of knitted stitches). I could put the crochet down and forget about it for several days, if need be, and still know exactly where I was when I returned to it. It's easy to correct mistakes, too: just unravel your work back to the misdemeanor in question, pick up the hook, and carry on.

Then came the apple cozies! In my search for an original Christmas gift for the children's teachers, I came across knitted cozies for fruit—knitted in the round on four needles. Well, it was challenging enough to knit with two needles, but four! Then my crochet came into its own. I sat with my cotton yarn, my apple, and my hook. A few hours later my first cozy was complete, finished with a button I had raided from Mom's button box. The rest, as they say, is history. I went from apple cozies to edgings for napkins and pillowcases to flowers galore; and all the while, granny squares were slowly piling up in the background. If I stumbled, Lena was always on hand to help. And it is amazing what you can find online these days—the worldwide craft community is quite literally at your fingertips.

I am constantly inspired by our life in the country, the coast, the woodland, and our ever-evolving garden. By contrast, my early working life was spent in the art, antique, and interiors trade in London. Now I am able to combine the two, bringing my knowledge of color, texture, and design to my crochet work. I like nothing more than trawling through the local auction house for old chairs, picture frames, or linens. Then I bring them back to the cottage

and start to work them into my scheme, whether it's giving the item a lick of paint or a crocheted edging; it all seems to come together with time. I derive equal pleasure from sitting in the kitchen, gazing out at the peonies and roses, dreaming up another project while the hens chatter away to each other in the background.

Crochet really is my rest and relaxation, time away from a busy work schedule, time to just sit quietly and be creative. Whether it's a soft kid mohair-silk scarf for a Christmas present or a seascape pillow crocheted with the leftovers, there is always a project in the pipeline. Crochet can give depth to a decorating scheme, a hint of color or an element of texture. It isn't just about blankets—it can add the little touches that finish a table setting or brighten a bathroom. It doesn't take much effort to get hooked on crochet, and I hope this collection of designs inspires you to scatter an eclectic assortment of crocheted treasures throughout your home.

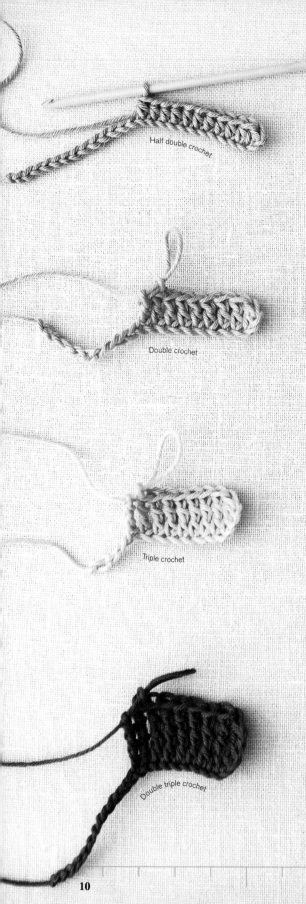

Half double crochet

Double crochet

Triple crochet

Double triple crochet

CROCHET BASICS

Crochet consists mainly of a series of loops, pulled through each other in various sequences. As with any craft, there are refinements to be mastered to achieve different effects, but the basic process is a simple one.

Materials

To start out on your crochet journey you simply need a selection of hooks (or just one for your first project), a good pair of scissors, tapestry needles (which have blunt points; a knitter's needle, or yarn needle, could also be used) for sewing in your ends, a tape measure, a notepad and pencil (I am forever making notes and writing down ideas I find elsewhere and my own ideas for using them), and, of course, some yarn.

Hooks

Hooks are available in metal, plastic, and a range of sustainable woods. Everyone will have their own preference, so try different ones until you find the most comfortable one for you. Secondhand stores are a good source of hooks and needles if you have the time to rummage. A pattern will suggest the best hook size for the required gauge. If you are designing your own crochet, you can use the size recommended on the yarn label as a guide, then make samples and change the hook size if necessary.

Yarn

It is no secret that I am passionate about natural fibers, but they can be expensive. For special or small projects they are ideal, but don't be afraid to substitute your own choice of yarn, such as a natural and synthetic mix, for the one I've suggested.

Holding the hook and yarn

How you hold the crochet hook and yarn is largely a matter of personal preference. I like to hold the hook like a knife, but you may prefer to hold it like a pencil instead. The yarn is held in your other hand, wound around your fingers in such a way that you can control its tension, so that it runs smoothly, but not loosely, as you work.

The picture below shows how I hold the yarn, but you can loop it around your fingers in any way that achieves the desired result.

If you are left-handed you'll probably want to hold the hook in your left hand and the yarn in your right. Hold the book up to a mirror to see how you can work crochet.

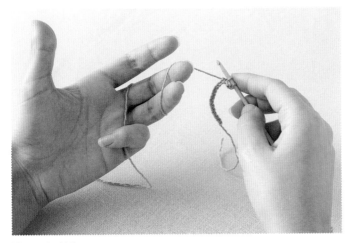

How to hold the yarn

How to hold the hook

Making a slip knot

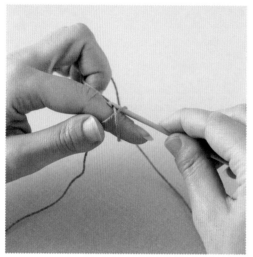

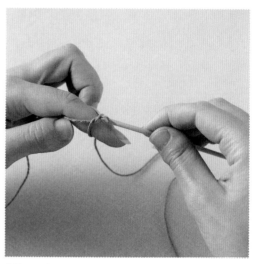

1 Most crochet starts with a slip knot. Make a loop around your finger with your yarn, crossing the yarn, then insert the hook into the loop.

2 Draw the yarn through and tighten it.

Abbreviations

ch	chain(s)
sl st	slip stitch
sc	single crochet
hdc	half double crochet
dc	double crochet
tr	triple
dtr	double triple
st(s)	stitch(es)

Chain stitch (ch)

Once the slip knot is on your hook, you can work the foundation chain, which is the basis for most pieces of crochet—the crochet equivalent of casting on in knitting. One or more chains also form part of many crochet stitch patterns.

Holding the working yarn taut, slide the hook under it from left to right, and as you do so, twist the hook counterclockwise, which draws the yarn under the hook itself. Pull the yarn through the slip knot. The loop you have just formed is your first chain. The pattern instructions will state how many chains you should make.

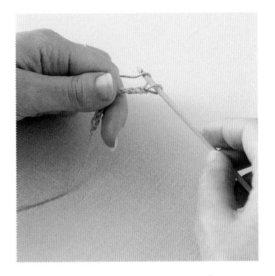

Slip stitch (sl st)

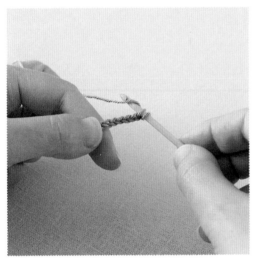

1 This is the most basic of all stitches, apart from a chain. The movement of picking up the yarn is often called "yarn over" (abbreviated to "yo") or in some books "yarn over hook" ("yoh"). Pass the hook through one stitch, picking up the yarn.

2 Then bring it back through that stitch and the one already on the hook in one movement.

Working in the round

If you are working in the round (to make a motif, for example), you need to start at the center. One way of doing this is to work just a few chains, join them to the slip knot with a slip stitch, and then work your first round of stitches over the chain loop. A better method, however, is to start with a slip ring, also called a magic circle. This is a somewhat tricky technique, but well worth mastering, as it ensures a neat, tight center for your work. You will first need to know how to work single crochet stitches (see page 15), so practice these on an ordinary row of crochet until you can work them without thinking. The basis of the ring is a slightly enlarged version of a slip knot.

Making a slip ring

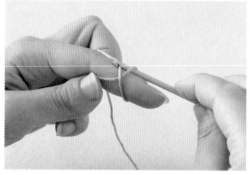

1 Hang the yarn over your index finger, the tail closest to you, and wrap the other end over your finger so that it crosses the tail. With the working (ball) yarn over your fingers, insert the hook under both strands of yarn where they cross and twist the hook clockwise over the working yarn.

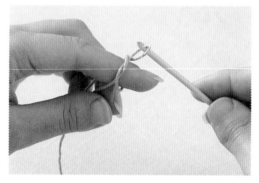

2 Pull a loop back under the ring into the center.

3 Now work a single chain stitch. Slide the loop off your finger, being careful not to close it. Work the stated number of stitches (here single crochet is shown) into the ring over both strands of yarn.

4 Pull on the tail end to close the circle, and continue working as instructed in the pattern.

Single crochet (sc)

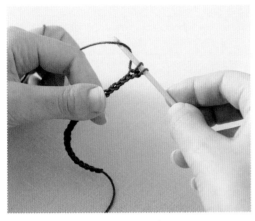 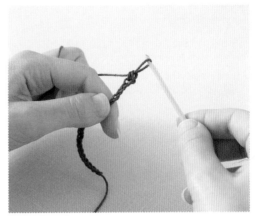

1 Pass the hook through the stitch on the previous row. This is normally done under both the front and back of the loop on the top of the stitch, unless stated otherwise. Pick up the yarn and bring it back through (at which point you will have two loops on your hook).

2 Hook the yarn again and bring it back through both of these loops at the same time. One loop remains on the hook and one single crochet stitch has been completed.

Half double crochet (hdc)

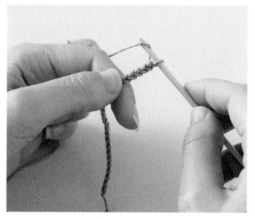

1 Wrap the yarn once around your hook, then pass the hook through the stitch to be worked into.

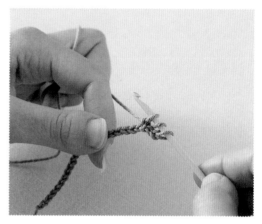

2 Hook the yarn and bring it back through. At this point you will have three loops on your hook: the loop from the original stitch, the extra loop made before inserting the hook, and the loop you have just picked up.

3 Hook the yarn again and draw it through all three loops at once. One loop remains on the hook and one half double stitch has been completed.

Double crochet (dc)

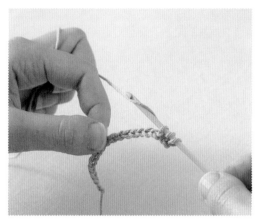

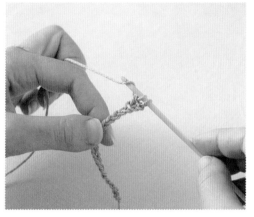

1 Wrap the yarn around your hook, then pass the hook through the stitch to be worked into. Hook the yarn and bring it back through. At this point you will have three loops on your hook: the loop from the original stitch, the extra loop made before inserting the hook, and the loop you have just picked up.

2 Hook the yarn again and draw it through the first two loops.

3 Hook it again and pass it through the remaining two loops. One loop remains on the hook and one double crochet has been completed.

Triple crochet (tr)

1 Wrap the yarn around your hook twice before passing it through the stitch to be worked into.

2 Hook the yarn and bring it back through. At this point you will have four loops on your hook: the original stitch, the two loops made by wrapping the yarn around the hook twice, and the loop you picked up before coming back through.

3 Hook the yarn again and draw it through the first two loops.

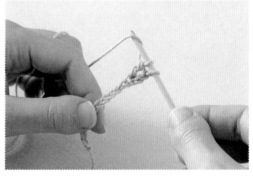

4 Hook it again and pass it through the second two loops.

5 Finally, hook the yarn and bring it back through the remaining two loops. One loop remains on the hook and one triple has been completed.

Double triple crochet (dtr)

1 Wrap the yarn around your hook three times before passing it through the stitch to be worked into.

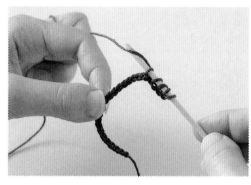

2 Hook the yarn and bring it back through. At this point you will have five loops on your hook.

3 Hook the yarn again and draw it through the first two loops. This will give you four loops on your hook.

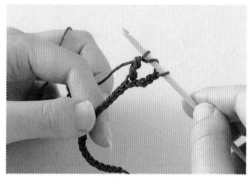

4 Hook it again and pass it through the second two loops.

5 Hook the yarn again and pass it through the third two loops.

6 Finally, hook the yarn and bring it back through the remaining two loops. One loop remains on the hook and one double triple has been completed.

Varying the texture

Normally, stitches are worked through both strands of the top loop of the stitch in the previous row. However, it is also possible to work into just the front part of the loop or just the back part. If you work into the back part of the loop (usually called "into back loop only"), this will produce a ridged effect on the right side of the work. If you work into the front part, a twisted line, resembling embroidered stem stitch, appears on the wrong side of the work.

Work into the back part of the loop to create a ribbed pattern. The finished effect can be seen on the yellow bathroom storage vessel (see page 97).

Adding height

Whether you are working backward and forward in rows or in the round, you will normally need to start each new row/round at the right level for the type of stitch that follows. This is achieved by working one or more chains at the end/beginning of each row. This is sometimes called a turning chain, as it precedes, or immediately follows, the turning of the work for a new row. I like the term "chain up" (followed by the number of chains to work), as it better conveys the purpose of the chain(s), especially when working in the round. Depending on the stitch you are using, you need to vary the number of chains you use:

sl st 1 chain
sc 1 chain
hdc 2 chains
dc 3 chains
tr 4 chains
dtr 5 chains

However, when I work in the round I tend not to work a turning chain; I simply go around and around. This is because I like the continuity of texture that this gives—in contrast to the line produced in the work by succeeding turning chains. But when following these patterns, please feel free to add a turning chain at the start of each round if you prefer. Either way, I think it is really useful to use a contrasting marker (see opposite) to indicate the start of your rounds. This is simply a short piece of contrasting yarn inserted at the beginning of each round.

Adding height for a new round

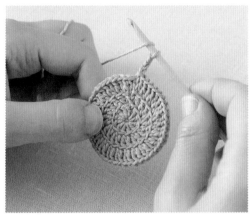

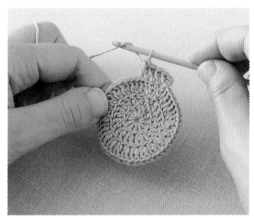

When adding height, the same technique applies whether you are working in the round or on rows. Here I am working in double crochet; therefore I have worked 3 chains to add height for my next round.

Once you have added height (your 3 chains will count as 1 dc), continue by working the first double crochet into the next stitch and continuing with doubles around or across your row.

Using a contrast marker when working in the round

To insert a contrasting marker between the last stitch of the previous round and the first stitch of the next, lay about 3 inches (8 cm) of yarn in a different color across your crochet before working the next stitch, then work over the top of it.

As you continue to work, move your marker up your rounds. This will enable you to keep sight of each completed round.

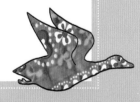

Increasing

The simplest way to increase in crochet is to work more than one stitch into a stitch in the previous row or round. The more extra stitches worked across a row, the more fullness will be created. If you work extra stitches at the beginning/end of rows you will produce an edge that slopes outward.

This example shows an increase being worked with three double crochet into a single stitch from the previous row, a technique beautifully illustrated by the Snowflake Scarf (see page 131).

Decreasing

The simplest form of decrease is to skip a stitch of the previous row or round—in effect, the reverse of the increasing method described above. Worked at intervals across one or more rows, it produces a fabric that draws inward.

A more usual method of decreasing is to work two stitches together to make one stitch. The precise method varies according to the stitch being used, but here is how you would decrease in single crochet. Insert your hook into the first stitch, yarn over and draw it through (2 loops on hook), insert it into next stitch, yarn over and draw it through again (3 loops on hook), yarn over and draw it through all 3 loops at once. Pattern instructions will normally give the exact sequence, set off by * * or ( ) to indicate that this is to be repeated every time the instruction to decrease a stitch appears. Decreases worked on a side edge will produce an edge that slopes inward.

This example shows a decrease being worked by crocheting 2 sc together.

Gauge

Pattern instructions will normally include a measurement of the gauge you will need to achieve if the work is to look like the item shown. This will usually be given as the number of stitches—and sometimes also rows—over a certain measurement, usually 4 inches (10 cm). In some cases the size of a small section of the pattern will be given, for comparison with the equivalent section you produce. The hook size is often specified, but this is only a guide. If you work loosely, you may need to change to a smaller hook; if you work tightly, you may need a larger one. For some of the designs in this book gauge is not critical, and this is stated on the pattern. Where the gauge is given, you should make a sample a little larger than the designated size and count the stitches (and sometimes rows) to check that your gauge is correct. This won't take long, and it could make a big difference to the quality of the finished work.

The gauge you produce is determined partly by your working tension—that is, how tightly or loosely you hold the yarn. As a beginner your tension may be unusually tight, because you are concentrating hard, or loose, because your are unsure. In time you'll achieve your own natural tension.

Fastening off

When you come to the end of a piece of crochet or the end of a specific color, cut your yarn, leaving enough to sew into the work, pull the end through the final stitch, and draw it up to close the loop.

To sew in the end, always use a needle of a size appropriate to your yarn; a tapestry needle (which has a blunt point) will go through the stitches without splitting them.

If you are working on a piece of crochet with a variety of colors, sew in your ends as you go along. There is nothing more daunting than a huge pile of sewing in at the end of a project.

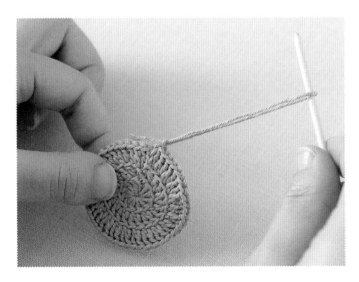

Pull the yarn through the final stitch until the end is released and ready to sew in. Then, using a needle, guide it through the top of the next stitch and into the body of your crochet to best conceal it.

Joining new yarn

To join a new yarn to the work, pull a loop of the yarn from back to front through a stitch of the previous row, then use this loop as the starting point for (usually) a single crochet. Once you have worked a few more stitches, sew the end into your work to fix it firmly.

When changing yarn colors for a granny square, I join the new yarn into a corner space, rather than a stitch, then chain up 2 and work the first group of corner stitches over the tail of the new yarn to secure it in place.

To join a new yarn to a piece of work, pull a loop through a stitch from the previous row. This technique is perfect for joining a new color to a solid piece of crochet.

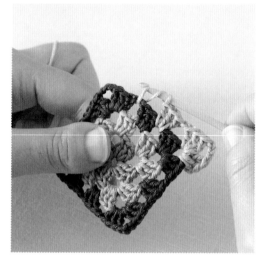

To change colors for a granny square, pull a loop through a corner space and work a single crochet over the chain corner, then continue with 2 chains to create your first double.

Pressing

Depending on the intended use of your crochet, it may need pressing. For example, if you need to attach it to fabric, press it first. Use an iron set to the appropriate heat for that yarn and place your work face down, so that if your iron has a tendency to mark, you won't ruin hours of hard work.

An even safer method is to place a press cloth (a clean dish towel or piece of fine linen) between your crochet and the iron;

this will protect the crochet and makes it safer to use steam, for a crisper finish. Not all crochet needs to be pressed, and if it is texture you are after, keep away from the iron.

One good tip for pressing a larger piece of crochet, such as a blanket, is to carefully place it under the mattress of a bed or under the cushions on your sofa—sitting or sleeping on it for a few days will press it beautifully.

Useful hand stitches

The following stitches are used in some of the projects in this book.

Slipstitch
Not to be confused with a crochet slip stitch (sl st), this is used to join two layers of fabric. It is worked in various ways, depending on the context, and in this book it is used several times to join a lining to an outer fabric. Fasten the thread at the right-hand edge of the work, in the outer layer, just under the folded edge of the lining. Bring the needle up into the fold of the lining, then take it down into the outer fabric immediately above this point; take it under this fabric (without going through to the outside) and then up through the fold of the lining. The stitches should be as small as possible and as close together as seems appropriate for the item (for example, about $^1/_8$ inch (2–3 mm) for the Smartphone Case and spaced more widely for the iPad Case).

Overcasting
Often used to finish a raw edge, this can be varied to join two sections of a toy, for example. Work from left to right, taking small vertical stitches through both sections and pulling fairly tightly to make the stitches as inconspicuous as possible.

Chain stitch
This embroidery stitch can be used to form a foundation for crochet, using the crochet yarn, as for the Pillowcase Edgings. Work from right to left. Bring the needle up at the starting point, make a small loop on the fabric, and take the needle back down at the point where it emerged. Holding the loop in place, bring the needle up a short distance away, over the loop, and pull the thread through. Repeat for the required distance. The size of the loops will vary according to the crochet you will be working. Make a small sample to decide on the finished effect.

Crochet with beads

For added texture and a bit of glamour,
beads are ideal. How you get the beads
onto the yarn depends on the relative sizes
of the yarn and beads. For some projects
you can simply thread the yarn into a needle
with a relatively large eye (such as a tapestry
needle) and slip the beads straight onto it.
If your beads have a small hole and your
thread is fine, you can use a beading needle,
as I did for the Pitcher Cover.

However, if you've got a fuzzy or thick yarn
and beads with small holes, you can try
the following method. First, cut a length of
sewing thread, double it and insert the loop
end through a beading needle (pulling the
loop longer than the two free ends). Then
insert the yarn end through the thread loop
and fold it back for a few inches. Pick up a
bead with the beading needle, slide it over
the combined 4 threads, then onto the loop,
then onto the loop of yarn. Pick up another
bead and repeat, sliding the first bead down
the single length of yarn (always keep one
bead on the yarn loop to hold it in place).
When all the beads are threaded, remove
the beading needle and thread. When
working the pattern, bring each bead
forward as needed.

Broomstick lace

This large-scale form of crochet is quick and satisfying to do. It was originally worked on a broomstick, but what you can use instead, along with your crochet hook, is a large knitting needle. The size of your needle will determine the size of the holes formed and the effect of your crochet. Always select your crochet hook to suit your yarn. For example, use a DK yarn with a size 35 knitting needle, but use an E / 4 or F / 5 (3.5 or 3.75 mm) crochet hook to work the stitches. The instructions below are for a basic broomstick loop stitch pattern.

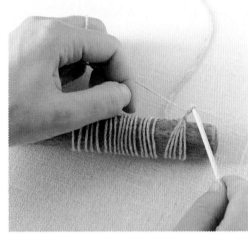

1 Start with a foundation chain using your crochet hook. Then, with the knitting needle in a firm position (some people, me included, like to hold it between their knees), hook the yarn through each chain and slip the loop onto the needle. Once you have worked across your foundation chain and looped all of your stitches onto your needle you are ready to start working them off again.

2 Using your crochet hook, hook the yarn through a group of 5 stitches with a single crochet.

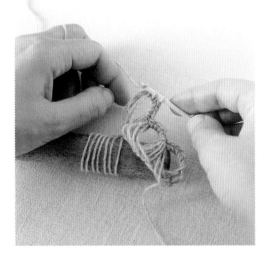

3 Once you have secured this group, slide it off the needle and crochet 4 more sc into the space in the center of the loops. Continue across the row in this way. Lengthen the last sc and slip it over the knitting needle. Through the top of each sc, hook the yarn back onto your needle. You are now ready to work the next row. This is worked in exactly the same way, without turning the work, as are the following rows.

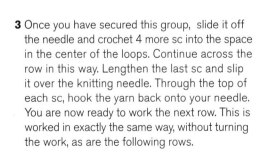

Tunisian crochet

This form of crochet (also called afghan stitch) is really effective if you want to create more substantial, textile-like crochet, for garments, bags, and the like. You will need a long Tunisian crochet hook, unless you are doing a very small piece of work, for which a regular crochet hook will be fine. This is the basic Tunisian simple stitch.

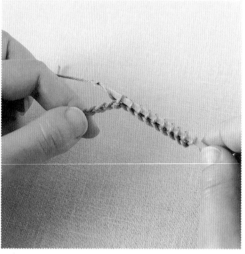

1 Start with a foundation chain as you would for regular crochet. Then, working back along your chain, insert your hook through each chain and pick up a loop. Don't work the stitches back off your hook—you will need a row of stitches on the hook, as in knitting. When you reach the end, do not turn but work 1 chain.

2 Hook your yarn and bring it back through the first 2 stitches, hook it again and repeat along the row, each time drawing the loop through 2 stitches, until you are left with just 1 stitch. Do not work a chain at this point.

3 Working in the opposite direction again, pass the hook through the vertical stitch and hook the yarn back, again leaving the new stitch on your hook. Continue along the row until you have a row of stitches on your hook. Maintaining the correct number of stitches on the hook, without increasing or decreasing by accident, can be tricky, but persevere and with practice you will crack it.

Crochet into fabric

I love to use crochet edgings to add detail to clothes and home accessories. Essentially, you are working a series of single crochets into the fabric, but pulling them long to accommodate the hem. You can simply press your hem in place and crochet over it, if you prefer not to have a stitched line. If you are working crochet into a closely woven fabric, you might prefer to embroider a line of chain stitch around the edge (see page 25) and then work the crochet stitches into the loops.

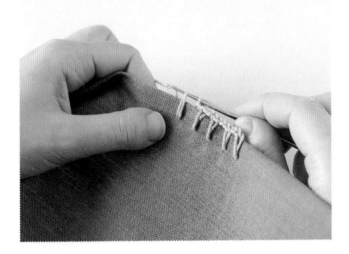

Each long single crochet is separated from the next by one or two chain stitches. The number of chain stitches you use will depend on the spacing you require.

KITCHEN

As a family, we tend to live in our kitchen: The
Sicilian can be cooking, the children sitting at
the table with their homework, and me, also
sitting at the table, but with a ball of yarn and
a crochet hook. By their nature and function,
kitchens tend to be cluttered, so to counteract
this, I have chosen to use neutral, natural
colours for the accessories in this chapter.
You can inject some color contrast with the
detail on your egg cozies, pot holders, or table
runner; just carry the same shades across the
various projects, rather than introducing too
many different ones. My palette is a fairly
muted one, but if you do want to introduce a
splash of color, use it as a reference point when
beginning each new project.

In my search for an original gift for Pipi's teacher, I came up with this pattern. An apple cozy is almost guaranteed to put a smile on someone's face. It might be in bemusement, or sheer delight at the thought of a cosseted apple in the bottom of a handbag, no longer battered or bruised by the house keys and other offending objects. I love crocheting these cozies (so much easier than knitting in the round, with the fiddly four needles)—it's very tactile and satisfying. I tend not to follow my pattern, but instead use an apple as my guide. Feel free to use a larger hook or different yarn: simply adjust the number of stitches accordingly— use an apple as your template and pull the cozy over it every so often to check that you are on the right track. Just remember that natural cotton has a good amount of stretch in it, so don't be afraid to squeeze in a slightly larger apple. For a fastening, you can use a new or vintage button. If you are feeling a bit more confident, crochet a tiny apple blossom in some fine cotton thread.

YOU WILL NEED

Cotton yarn, such as Rowan Cotton Glacé, Rowan Milk Cotton DK or Sublime Soya Cotton DK: 1 x 50 g (1¾ oz) ball is enough for 3 cozies

Crochet hook: 3.5 mm or E / 4

Tapestry needle

1 button (new or vintage) for each cozy

For apple blossom (optional): small amount of fine crochet thread, such as DMC Crochet Cotton no. 80, in pink and white

Crochet hook: 0.75 mm or 12 steel

Sewing needle

GAUGE

Gauge is not critical for this project.

FINISHED SIZE

To fit a medium-size apple

LEVEL

Starting out The repetitive nature of this pattern is good for reinforcing your command of the basic single crochet stitch. And going around and around in circles, with the occasional increase and decrease, is reassuringly simple.

INSTRUCTIONS

I have worked into the outside, or back, loop of the stitch (the one farther away from you) to create the smooth effect on the right side when working in rounds. You can create different effects by working into the front of the loop or through both loops at the same time.

Ch 4, join with a sl st into first ch to form a ring.
Round 1 ch 1, 9 sc into ring, sl st into first ch.
Round 2 2 sc into back loop only of each st (18 sts). (Remember to work all sc into back loop only.) Insert a contrasting yarn marker (positioned horizontally between the last stitch and the first one of the next round) at this point; this will allow you to see when you have completed a round and eliminates the need to count stitches. Move it up your cozy on every round as you work.
Round 3 1 sc into each st.
Round 4 * 2 sc into next st, 1 sc into following st *, repeat from * to * to marker.
Round 5 repeat round 3.
Round 6 * 2 sc into next st, 1 sc into each of following 2 sts *, repeat from * to * to marker.
Rounds 7 and 8 repeat round 3.
Round 9 * 2 sc into next st, 1 sc into each of following 4 sts *, repeat from * to * to marker (don't worry if there aren't exactly 4 stiches in the final group).
Rounds 10 and 11 repeat round 3.
At the end of round 11, turn work and begin working backward and forward in rows for the opening at the top of the cozy.
Row 1 (right side) ch 1, 1 sc into front loop only of each st to end, turn.
Row 2 ch 1, 1 sc into back loop only of each st to end, turn.
Row 3 ch 1, * 1 sc into front loop only of each of the next 5 sts, skip 1 st *, repeat from * to * to end of row (don't worry if there aren't exactly 5 stitches in the final group), turn.
Row 4: ch 1, 1 sc into back loop only of each st to end, turn.

Row 5: ch 1, 1 sc into front loop only of each st to end. At the end of row 5, ch 10, sl st in last sc to form a loop for the button. Fasten off. Sew the button to the cozy opposite the loop.

If you would like a larger cozy, just work 1 or more extra increase rounds (2 sc into next st at regular intervals) at the beginning and more decrease rows (skipping every 6th st) at the end, and add a few extra straight rounds in the middle.

For crocheted apple blossom
Round 1 start with a slip ring using pink thread. 1 sc into ring, followed by ch 2 (counts as 1 dc), 9 dc into ring, sl st into top of 2 ch. Pull the ring tight. Fasten off.
Round 2 attach the white thread to back edge of dc, * 1sc, 3 dc and 1 sc all into next st, sl st into following st *, repeat from * to * to end, sl st in first sc. (You will have 5 petals.) Fasten off.

With 15 hens and roosters now roaming free at Number One Churchill's Green, I take pure delight in anything egg related. Since I bought the first three hens for The Sicilian as an anniversary gift two years ago, we have acquired a variety of chicks, bantams and rescue birds, not to mention hatching out several of our very own chicks. I thought it only right to do their beautiful free-range eggs justice; hence these cotton cozies. Use your imagination to make handles for them; you can use buttons or even little scraps of fabric, but do try the bugle flowers. These can be used to decorate all sorts of objects—make some and keep them on hand for gift wrapping, for example.

YOU WILL NEED

Craft cotton, such as Stylecraft Craft Cotton in Ecru: 1 x 100 g (3½ oz) ball is more than enough for all 6 cozies

Small amounts of contrasting yarn for trimming; I used Debbie Bliss Bella, shade 014 Duck Egg, and Debbie Bliss Eco, shade 603 Gold: 1 x 50 g (1¾ oz) ball of either is more than enough to decorate all of the cozies

Crochet hook: 2.25 mm or B / 1

Tapestry needle

For trimmings: vintage buttons; cotton fabric scraps; bugle flowers

GAUGE

22 sc and 24 rows to 4 inches (10 cm)

FINISHED SIZE

To fit a large egg

LEVEL

Starting out This pattern is similar to the apple cozy pattern but a little simpler, so is perfect for beginners.

INSTRUCTIONS

Round 1 Start with a slip ring, ch 1, 11 sc into the ring, pull ring tight, sl st into first ch to close the ring.
Work with wrong side facing, working into back loop only of each st throughout.
Round 2 ch 1, 2 sc into each of 11 sts (22 sts). Place a contrasting marker at this point (and move marker up at end of each round) to indicate the start of each following round.
Round 3 * 2 sc into next st, 1 sc into next st *, repeat from * to * to end (33 sts).
Round 4 1 sc into each sc to end.
Rounds 5–12 repeat round 4.
Join round 12 with a sl st into first sc. Fasten off. Turn right side out.
Using a contrasting color, join the yarn to any st of round 12; ch 1, 2 sc into both loops of each stitch to end. By

doubling the stitches, you will create the bell-like lower edge of the cozy. If you prefer straight sides, just work 1 sc into each stitch. Fasten off. Attach a button, a flower, or a little loop of fabric to serve as a handle for your egg cozy.

Bugle flower

Round 1 Start with a slip ring, 10 sc into ring, then pull tight and sl st in first sc.
Round 2 (petals) * ch 4, 7 tr into next sc, turn petal to the back and sl st into top of 4 ch to form trumpet shape, ch 4, turn to right side, sl st into next sc *, repeat from * to * 4 times, working last sl ss into first sc of round 1. Fasten off.

I have a rather eclectic mix of pot holders, received as gifts over the years. In an effort to bring a more coherent scheme to my chaotic kitchen, I thought I'd try making a collection of them in matching colours. I used "craft" or "dishcloth" cotton yarn, which is inexpensive and sturdy, but you can use any medium-weight smooth-finish yarn in contrasting colors to suit your kitchen's décor.

YOU WILL NEED

Medium-weight cotton yarn in ecru: 1 x 100 g (3½ oz) ball is ample for all three pot holders

Contrasting yarn, such as Rowan Cotton Glacé or Debbie Bliss Eco Aran Fair Trade Collection: 1 x 50 g (1¾ oz) ball

Crochet hook: 4 mm or G / 6

Tapestry needle

Safety pins

GAUGE

Gauge is not critical for this project.

FINISHED SIZE

Pot holder with stripe about 6 x 6 inches (15 x 15 cm)

Flower-shaped pot holder about 6 inches (15 cm) in diameter

Granny squares pot holder about 6 x 6 inches (15 x 15 cm)

LEVEL

Moving on These pot holders aren't complicated, but they do introduce some new stitches, so give them a try if you feel ready to move forward with your crochet. This cotton is so easy and quick to work with that if you make a mistake you won't mind undoing it and trying again.

INSTRUCTIONS

Pot holder with stripe

Using main color, ch 37.

Foundation row 2 hdc tog in 3rd and 4th ch from hook.
* ch 1, 2 hdc tog into next 2 ch *, repeat from * to * to last
ch, 1 hdc into last ch, turn.

Row 1 ch 2, 2 hdc tog in first and 2nd ch spaces * ch 1,
2 hdc tog in same ch space as last st and in next ch
space *, repeat from * to * to end, ch 1, 1 hdc into top of
turning ch, turn.

Rows 2–4 repeat row 1.

Rows 5 and 6 using contrasting color, repeat row 1.

Rows 7–11 using main color, repeat row 1.

At the end of row 7, ch 14, sl st into first ch to make
a loop for hanging. Fasten off.

Flower-shaped pot holder

Round 1 Using main color, start with a slip ring. ch 1,
9 sc into ring, pull tight to close ring, sl st into first ch.

Round 2 ch 1, 2 sc into each sc, sl st into 1 ch (18 sc).

Round 3 ch 1, * 1 sc and 2 dc into next sc, skip 1 sc *,
repeat from * to * to end, sl st into 1 ch.

Round 4 ch 1, * 1 sc and 2 dc into next sc, skip 2 dc *,
repeat from * to * to end, sl st into 1 ch.

Round 5 using contrasting color, ch 1, * 2 sc into next sc,
1 sc into each of next 2 dc *, repeat from * to * to end, sl
st into 1 ch (36 sc).

Round 6 using contrasting color, repeat round 3.

Round 7 using main color, ch 1, * skip next sc, 1 sc and
3 dc into next dc, skip next dc *, repeat from * to * to end,
sl st into 1 ch.

Round 8 using main color, ch 1, * skip next sc, 1 sc and
3 dc into next dc, skip next dc *, repeat from * to * to end,
sl st into 1 ch.

Round 9 repeat round 8.

Round 10 repeat round 8 but work 4 dc instead of 3 dc
each time. At the end of round 10, ch 14, sl st into first ch
to make a loop for hanging. Fasten off.

Granny squares pot holder

Make 9 mini granny squares as follows.

Using main color, ch 4, sl st into first ch to form
a ring.

Round 1 working into ring, ch 3 (counts as 1 dc), 2 dc
(each group of 3 dc forms one side of mini square), ch 3
(to form corner), 3 dc (side 2), ch 3, 3 dc (side 3), ch 3, 3
dc (side 4), ch 3 (to form last corner), sl st into 3rd of 3 ch.

Round 2 ch 1, 1 sc into each of next 2 dc, *2 sc, ch 1,
2 sc* into corner space, continue around the square with
1 sc into each dc and from * to * into each corner space,
sl st into 1 ch. Fasten off.

To join the squares, use contrasting color and follow the
instructions for the Granny Square Blanket on page 107.

To work the border, using contrasting color, work 1 sc all
the way around the edge, working 1 sc, ch 1 and 1 sc
into each corner space, sl st into first sc. Fasten off. Using
main color, join the yarn in a corner space, ch 2 (counts
as 1 hdc), 1 hdc, ch 1, 2 hdc, all in corner space, continue
round with 1 hdc into each stitch and working each corner
with 2 hdc, ch 1, 2 hdc, sl st into 2nd of 2 ch.

At the end of the border, ch 14, sl st into first ch to make
a loop for hanging. Fasten off.

SQUAB CUSHION WITH CROCHETED BUTTONS

This is such a simple but effective project. Choose a solid-color and a patterned fabric to match your chairs or kitchen and you've got two schemes in one. Select your yarn accordingly: go for a contrast (as bright as you like) for one side and a harmonizing color on the other. As usual, I've opted for solid-color linen on one side, giving a little texture, complemented by a pretty printed Tilda cotton on the other. These crocheted buttons can be used to decorate clothing, bags and anything else that comes to mind. Each cushion needs 10 buttons—5 on each side.

YOU WILL NEED

Washable cotton yarn, such as Twilley's Freedom Sincere Organic Cotton DK or Rowan Cotton Glacé: 1 x 50 g (1¾ oz) ball is sufficient for 12 buttons; divide the total number of buttons required by 12 to determine the number of balls required

Crochet hook: 2.25 mm or B / 1

Polyester batting of desired thickness for pillow forms; measure chair seat and multiply area by number of cushions

Linen or cotton fabric for cushion cover; for each side, measure as for batting, then add 2 inches (5 cm) seam allowance to each dimension (so, for a 12- x 14-inch [30- x 36- cm] cushion, you would need pieces measuring 14 x 16 inches [35 x 41 cm]). Add fabric for ties (4 for each cushion); these measure, finished, 15 inches (38 cm) long and ¾ inch (2 cm) wide; double the width measurement and add 2 inches (5 cm) to each dimension

Strong sewing thread to match buttons (choose a harmonizing neutral shade for these unless they are all the same color)

Ordinary sewing thread to match or harmonize with fabrics

Sewing machine (optional) or ordinary sewing needle

Tapestry needle

Large chenille needle or other sharp-pointed needle

Steel tape measure

Water-erasable pen

GAUGE

Gauge is not critical for this project.

FINISHED SIZE

Each button measures about 1¼ inches (3 cm) in diameter.

LEVEL

Starting out These crocheted buttons are a very simple project.

INSTRUCTIONS

Ch 6, sl st into first ch to form a ring. Buttons are worked with wrong side facing.
Round 1 ch 1, 11 sc into ring, sl st into first ch.
Work into back loop only of each st throughout.
Round 2 ch 1, * 2 sc into next st, 1 sc into following st *, repeat from * to * to end, sl st into 1 ch.
Round 3 ch 3 (counts as 1 sc, plus 2 ch), 1 sc into next st, * ch 2, 1 sc into following st *, repeat from * to * to last st, ch 2, sl st into first of 3 ch. Fasten off.

To finish

Measure and cut out a top and bottom piece of fabric for each cushion, remembering to add 2 inches (5 cm) to each dimension. Cut 4 strips of fabric for ties, twice the desired finished width plus 2 inches (5 cm) in both dimensions for seam allowances. Cut a piece of batting the desired finished size of the cushion.

Fold each strip along its length with right sides facing. Stitch along the length, 1 inch (2.5 cm) from the raw edges, using a sewing machine (or needle and thread and small backstitches). Trim the seam allowances to ¼ inch (5 mm) and press them open. Move the seam to the center and stitch across one end. Trim the seam allowances as before and press this seam flat. Turn the strip right side out, using a knitting needle or pencil, and press it flat. Make 4 ties for each cushion.

Pin the two cushion pieces together with right sides facing and edges matching. Using a water-erasable pen and a tape measure (or a ruler), mark the stitching line 1 inch (2.5 cm) from the raw edges along the front and two side edges. Pin two ties just inside this line at each back corner, matching all raw edges so the ties lie within the main area of the cushion. Stitch around the three edges; press the seam flat. Trim the seam allowances to ½ inch (1 cm), then trim diagonally across the front edge corners to reduce bulk.

Turn the cover right side out, pushing the corners out gently, then insert the pillow form. (If it doesn't fit easily, remove it and trim the edges slightly.) Fold in the two free edges of the cover and pin them together. Topstitch these edges together, catching in the ties and stitching as close as possible to the edges for a crisp finish.

Using a steel tape measure (or a ruler) and a water-erasable pen, mark two diagonal lines from corner to corner, then draw a rectangle joining these diagonals and the chosen distance for the 4 outer buttons. Thread the chenille needle with sewing thread and fasten it at the crossing point of the two diagonals; thread it through the center of a button, then take the needle straight down through the batting and other fabric. Thread it through a button, then take it back to the first side, pulling tightly on the thread to produce a deep-buttoned effect. Repeat these two movements 8–10 times. If you take care to stitch between—not over—the crochet stitches, the sewing stitches should be invisible. Fasten off the thread securely just under the center of a button.

Repeat with the remaining 8 buttons, positioning them where the rectangle crosses the diagonal lines. Rinse away the water-erasable pen marks.

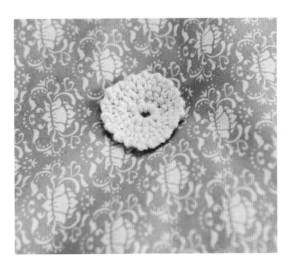

The inspiration for this piece comes from a beautiful old centerpiece I found in an antique shop. I was intrigued by the intricacy of the overlapping lace bands, and together with my friend Lena I analyzed the stitches behind this pattern. This project is the crochet equivalent of a carefully handcrafted piece of reproduction furniture, true to the original in style and craftmanship. Although the pattern is less complicated than you might think at first glance, this is a challenging piece and will require some time to complete—time well spent, I think, to produce what may become an heirloom of the future. I chose to do the project in a classic linen thread.

YOU WILL NEED

Anchor Artiste Linen Crochet Thread, shade 392 Ecru (or other 10-count linen crochet thread): 1 x 50 g (1¾ oz) ball

Crochet hook: 1 mm or 11 steel

Tapestry needle

GAUGE

25 sc and 20 rows to 4 inches (10 cm)

FINISHED SIZE

The centerpiece measures about 14½ x 12 inches (37 x 30 cm).

LEVEL
Confident

INSTRUCTIONS

Motif 1

Round 1 start with a slip ring, 1 sc, ch 2 (counts as 1 dc), 39 dc into slip ring, sl st into top of 2 ch.

Round 2 ch 3 (counts as 1 dc), 1 dc into each of next 3 sts; * ch 3, 1 dc into each of next 4 sts, *, repeat from * to * end, ch 3, sl st into top of 3 ch (10 groups).

Round 3 sl st into back loop only of next 3 dc, 1 sc, ch 2 (counts as 1 dc) into first ch space, 2 dc, ch 3 and 3 dc into same ch space, ch 3, * 3 dc, ch 3 and 3 dc into next 3-ch space, ch 3 *, repeat from * to * to end, sl st into top of 2 ch.

Round 4 sl st into back loop only of next 2 dc, 1 sc, ch 2 (counts as 1 dc) in first ch space, 2 dc, ch 3 and 3 dc in same ch space, ch 2, 1 sc in next 3-ch space, ch 2, * 3 dc, ch 3 and 3 dc into next ch space, ch 2, 1 sc in next 3-ch space, ch 2 *, repeat from * to * to end, sl st into top of 2 ch.

Round 5 2 sl st into back loop only of next 2 dc and into first ch space, 1 sc into ch space, * ch 12, 1 sc into next 3-ch space *, repeat from * to * to end, ch 12, sl st into first sc.

Round 6 1 sc, ch 2 (counts as 1 dc) into first ch space, 13 dc into same ch space, 14 dc into each of next three ch spaces, 13 dc into next ch space, 14 dc into each of next four ch spaces, 13 dc into last ch space, sl st into top of 2 ch.

Round 7 ch 5 (counts as 1 dc and 2 ch), skip 1 st, 1 dc into back loop only of next dc, * ch 2, skip 1 st, 1 dc into back loop only of next st, *, repeat from * to * to end, ch 2, sl st into 3rd of 5 ch.

Round 8 ch 5 (counts as 1 dc and 2 ch), * 1 dc into next dc, ch 2 *, repeat from * to * to end, sl st into 3rd of 5 ch.

Round 9 1 sc, ch 2 (counts as 1 dc) into first ch space, 2 dc, ch 3 and 3 dc into same ch space, ch 4, * skip next two ch spaces, 3 dc, ch 3 and 3 dc in next ch space, ch 4 *, repeat from * to * to end, sl st into top of 2 ch.

Round 10 sl st into each of next 2 dc, 1 sc, ch 2 (counts as 1 dc) into first ch space, 2 dc, ch 3 and 3 dc into same ch space, ch 6, * 3 dc, ch 3 and 3 dc into next 3-ch space, ch 6 *, repeat from * to * to end, sl st into top of 2 ch.

Round 11 sl st into each of next 2 dc, 1 sc, ch 2 (counts as 1 dc) into first ch space, 2 dc into same ch space, ch 32, 1 dc into 4th ch from hook, 1 dc into each of next 28 ch (first lace formed), 3 dc into same ch space as last 2 dc, ch 3, 1 sc around 4-ch space of round 9 and 6-ch space of round 10, ch 3, * 3 dc into next 3-ch space, ch 32, 1 dc into 4th ch from hook, 1 dc into each of next 28 ch (second lace formed), 3 dc into same 3-ch space as last 3 dc, ch 3, 1 sc around 4-ch space and 6-ch space

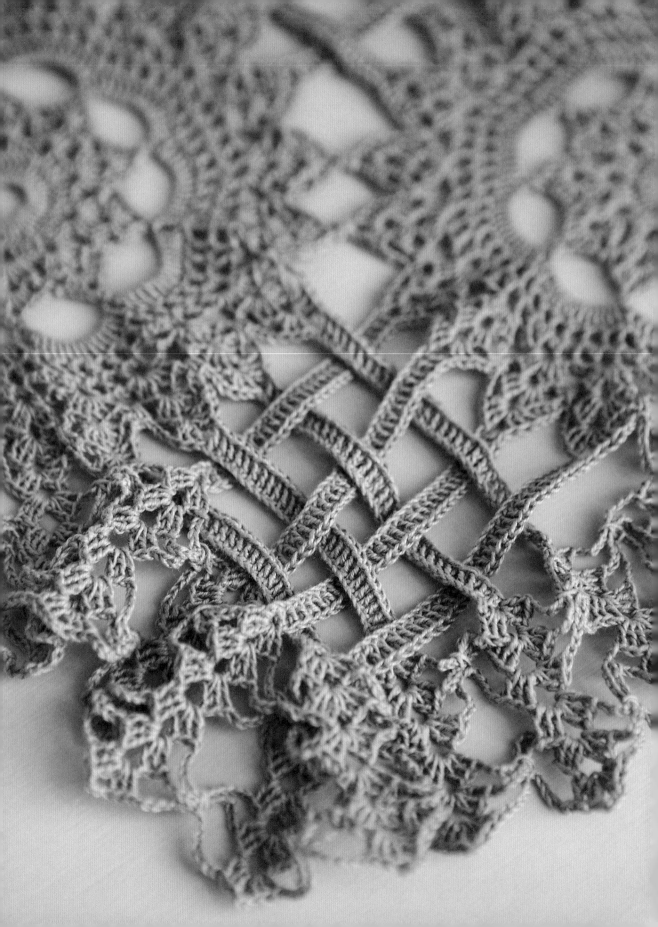

below, ch 3 *, repeat from * to * 2 more times to give a total of 4 laces, ** 3 dc, ch 3 and 3 dc into next 3-ch space, ch 3, 1 sc around 4-ch space and 6-ch space below, ch 3 (first petal without lace extension complete) **, repeat from ** to ** once to complete second petal without lace extension, repeat from * to * 4 times, repeat from ** to ** 13 times, sl st into top of 2 ch. Fasten off.

Motif 2

Work as for motif 1 to end of round 10.

Round 11 work as round 11 of motif 1, but when working from ** to ** for the first and second time, join to corresponding petal without lace extension on motif 1 by replacing the 3 ch at the center of the petal with ch 1, 1 sc in space at center of corresponding petal on motif 1, ch 1. Fasten off.

Motifs 1 and 2 combined

Note Place motifs side by side on a table with laces at center top and center bottom. Beginning at center top, weave the four laces from motif 1 alternately under and over the four laces from motif 2. Hold them in place with safety pins. I like the centerpiece to be quite frilly, but if you would prefer this part of it to be less voluminous, reduce the number of chains between the 3 dc, ch 3, 3 dc repeat at the top of the laces on rounds 12, 13, 14, 15, and 16.

Round 12 attach yarn in the 3-ch space of the last petal without lace extension at the right of the top laces, 1 sc, ch 2 (counts as 1 dc) in 3-ch space, 2 dc, ch 3 and 3 dc in same 3-ch space, ch 10, * 3 dc, ch 3 and 3 dc in ch space at end of first lace, ch 10 *, repeat from * to * into each of remaining 7 laces at top, repeat from * to * into 3-ch space at center of each petal to next group of laces, repeat from * to * into each lace, repeat from * to * into 3-ch space at center of each petal, sl st into 2nd of 2 ch.

Round 13 sl st into each of next 2 dc, 1 sc, ch 2 (counts as 1 dc) into first 3-ch space, 2 dc, ch 3 and 3 dc into same space, ch 10, * 3 dc, ch 3 and 3 dc into next 3-ch space, ch 10 *, repeat from * to * to end, sl st into 2nd of 2 ch.

Round 14 sl st into each of next 2 dc, 1 sc, ch 2 (counts as 1 dc) into first 3-ch space, 2 dc, ch 3 and 3 dc into same space, ch 5, 1 sc around both 10-ch spaces below, ch 5, * 3 dc, ch 3 and 3 dc into next 3-ch space, ch 5, 1 sc around both 10-ch spaces below, ch 5 *, repeat from * to * to end, sl st into 2nd of 2 ch.

Round 15 repeat round 13, but work ch 12 instead of ch 10 each time.

Round 16 repeat round 13, but work ch 13 instead of ch 10 each time.

Round 17 repeat round 14, but work ch 6, 1 sc around 12-ch space and 13-ch space below, ch 6 between petals. Fasten off.

Carefully lay the centerpiece out and press it flat, using a pressing cloth. There is some overlap at the top of the laces; position these as you prefer before pressing.

A couple of years ago I came across a Debbie Bliss pattern for knitted cotton shelf edging. It still graces my long kitchen shelf and has been washed several times to keep it fresh and white. This simple crocheted edging can add an accent of texture or color to bookshelves, kitchen shelving, dressers, or window frames. I've opted for a neutral cream, but am tempted now to do some bright pink and orange edging for Pipi's room, it's so quick and easy.

YOU WILL NEED

Cotton yarn, DK weight, such as Puppets Lyric 8/8 Crochet & Knitting Cotton, shade 5002 Cream: 1 x 50 g (1¾ oz) ball (70 m/76 yards) is enough to make the edgings illustrated; for additional length you will need to calculate the amount of yarn needed

Crochet hook: 3.5 mm or E / 4

Tapestry needle

GAUGE

Gauge is not critical for this project, but you should get about 6 pattern repeats to 4 inches (10 cm); each repeat measures about ⅝ x 1¼ inches (1.5 x 3 cm).

FINISHED SIZE

The edging shown, based on 163 ch, measures 34½ inches (88 cm) long.

LEVEL

Starting out It's very satisfying to work on such a simple "instant" project.

INSTRUCTIONS

Ch 163 (or the number required for your shelf; use Finished Size, above, to calculate the number).
Row 1 1 sc into 2nd ch from hook, 1 sc into each ch to end, turn.
Row 2 ch 1, 1 sc into back loop only of each st to end, turn.
Row 3 ch 3, * skip 2 sts, 1 dc into next sc, ch 2 and then work 3 dc around stem of last dc *, repeat from ** to **, ch 2, sl st into last st. Fasten off.

Variation

Using just one ball, I had only enough yarn to do one full edging, as described above, so for the second edging I simply removed row 2 from the pattern.

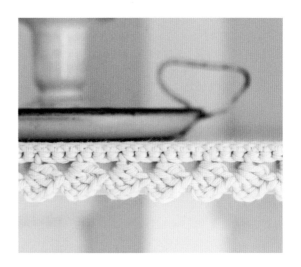

This is the perfect way to use up your threads or gather together some of the motifs you've made over a few months. I've combined motifs from two other patterns, together with two new ones, using a total of 16 motifs; if your table runner is larger or smaller you may wish to use a different number. (And, of course, you can use your own choice of colors.) This runner is perfect for a dining table, dotted with bud vases, bowls of antipasti and bottles of chilled vino—happy days!

YOU WILL NEED

Crochet cottons in the following types and colors:

Blue motifs: Anchor Aida 6-ply Crochet Cotton, no. 10, shade 0850: 1 x 50 g (1¾ oz) ball

Pink motifs: Anchor Artiste Mercer Crochet Cotton, no. 20, shade 893: 1 x 20 g ball

Purple motifs: Anchor Pearl Cotton, no. 8, shade 871: 1 x 10 g ball

Natural linen motifs: Anchor Artiste Linen Crochet Thread, no. 10, shade 392: 1 x 50 g (1¾ oz) ball

Green motifs: Anchor Pearl Cotton, no. 8, shade 265: 1 x 10 g ball

Cotton table runner: the purchased one shown measures 79 x 16 inches (200 x 40 cm); alternatively, make your own, from 2 yards (2 m) of cotton or linen fabric, using the excess for napkins.

Crochet hook: 1.25 mm or 7 steel

Tapestry needle

Sewing needle

Crewel or chenille needle

Sewing thread in a neutral shade

Water-erasable pen

GAUGE

Gauge is not crucial for this project.

FINISHED SIZE

The runner measures about 79 x 16 inches (200 x 40 cm).

LEVEL

Confident There is quite a lot going on here, but if you're feeling confident, give it a try. I have varied the motifs here from their originals by working into both loops on some and just the back loops on others. Once you are feeling more confident with your own skills, why not experiment a little with the different effects you can create by doing the same?

INSTRUCTIONS

THE MOTIFS

To embellish your table runner as shown here, you will need assorted motifs, including patterns from two other projects in this book: the Summer Lawn Handbag (see pages 122–5) and the Smartphone Case (see pages 126–9).

- Handbag, pink flower, work 1 x green, 1 x purple, 1 x natural linen
- Handbag, large green flower, work 1 x pink, 1 x green
- Handbag, smaller green flower, work 1 x blue
- Handbag, turquoise flower, work 1 x blue and 1 x natural linen
- Case, small pink, work 1 x pink
- Case, blue, work 1 x green & 1 x purple
- Case, pale green, work 1 x pink

You will also need 3 new motifs using the patterns given below.

Large purple motif

(Make 1 in purple.)

Round 1 start with a slip ring, 1 sc into ring and ch 2 (counts as 1 dc), work 15 dc into ring, sl st into top of 2 ch. Pull tail of thread to close ring (16 sts).

Round 2 ch 2 (counts as 1 sc, 1 ch), work 1 sc and ch 1 into each dc of previous round, sl st into first ch.

Round 3 into next ch space, 1 sc, ch 5 (counts as 1 dc, 3 ch), * 1 dc into next ch space, ch 3 *, repeat from * to *, sl st into 2nd of 5 ch.

Round 4 into next ch space, 1 sc, ch 4 (counts as 1 dc, 2 ch), 1 dc into same ch space, * 1 dc, ch 2 and 1 dc into next ch space *, repeat from * to *, sl st into 2nd of 4 ch.

Round 5 into next ch space, 1 sc, ch 2 (counts as 1 dc), 1 dc, ch 2, 2 dc into same ch space, * 2 dc, ch 2 and 2 dc into next ch sp *, repeat from * to *, sl st into top of 2 ch.

Round 6 1 sl st into top of next st, 1 sc into ch space, ch 8 (counts as 1 tr, 5 ch), 1 tr into same ch sp, * 1 tr, ch 5 and 1 tr into next ch space, *, repeat from * to *, sl st into 3rd of 8 ch.

Round 7 1 sc into next ch space, ch 4 (counts as 1 dtr), 2 dtr, ch 2 and 3 dtr into same ch space, * 3 dtr, ch 2 and 3 dtr into next ch sp *, repeat from * to *, sl st into top of 4 ch.

Round 8 * 1 sc into each of 3 dtr, 2 sc into ch space, ch 3, 1 sc into same ch space, 1 sc into each of next 3 dtr, sl st between this group of dtr and next group *, repeat from * to *, sl st into first sc. Fasten off.

Large open motif

(Make 1 in natural linen thread, 1 in green.)

Round 1 start with a slip ring, 1 sc, ch 3 (counts as 1 tr) into ring, 17 tr into ring, sl st into top of 3 ch (18 sts). Pull tail of thread to close ring.

Round 2 ch 4 (counts as 1 dc, 1 ch), 1 dc and ch 1 into each tr, sl st into 3rd of 4 ch.

Round 3 1 sc into next ch space, ch 3 (counts as 1 tr), ch 2, 1 tr into same ch space, * ch 2, 2 tr into next ch space *, repeat from * to *, ch 2, sl st into top of 3 ch.

Round 4 sl st into next tr and into ch space, 1 sc, ch 2 (counts as 1 dc), 1 dc into same ch space, * ch 3, 2 dc into next ch space *, repeat from * to *, ch 3, sl st into top of 2 ch.

Round 5 sl st into next dc, 1 sc into ch sp, ch 2 (counts as 1 dc), 1 dc, ch 2, 2 dc into same ch space, * 2 dc, ch 2 and 2 dc into next ch sp *, repeat from * to *, sl st into top of 2 ch.

Round 6 repeat round 5.

Round 7 sl st across into next dc, 1 sc into ch space, ch 3 (counts as 1 tr), 1 tr, ch 3, 2 tr into same ch space, * 2 tr, ch 3 and 2 tr into next ch sp *, repeat from * to *, sl st into top of 3 ch.

Round 8 repeat round 7, but work ch 4 instead of ch 3 between pairs of tr.

Round 9 ch 1, * 1 sc into top of each of next 2 tr, 2 sc, ch 3 and 2 sc into ch space, 1 sc into each of next 2 tr, sl st between these 2 tr and next 2 tr *, repeat from * to *, sl st into 1 ch. Fasten off.

Scalloped flower motif

(Make 1 in blue.)

Round 1 start with a slip ring, 1 sc, ch 2 (counts as 1 dc) into ring, 11 dc, sl st into top of 2 ch, pull tail to close ring.

Round 2 1 sc into top of 2 ch, ch 2 (counts as 1 dc), 1 dc into same st, 2 dc into each dc, sl st into top of 2 ch.

Round 3 ch 1, * ch 5, skip 1 st, 1 sc into next st *, repeat from * to *, ending ch 5, skip last st, first ch.

Round 4 sl st into first 2 ch to reach the center of the ch space, 1 sc into center of ch space, * ch 5, 1 sc into center of next ch space *, repeat from * to *, ending ch 5, sl st into first sc.

Round 5 repeat round 4, but with 6 ch between each sc.

Round 6 sl st into first 3 ch, 1 sc into center of ch, * ch 7, 1 sc into center of next ch space *, repeat from * to *, ending ch 7, sl st into first sc.

Round 7 sl st into first 3 ch, 1 sc into center of ch space, * ch 9, 1 sc into center of next ch space *, repeat from * to *, ending ch 9, sl st into first sc.

Round 8 ch 3, 8 dc into first ch space, 9 dc into each ch, sl st into top of 3 ch. Fasten off.

To finish

Position your motifs on your runner and pin them in place. Using a neutral thread (or, if you prefer, a shade similar to that of the motif), sew each motif in place by hand. I like to work my stitches following the crochet rounds, starting at the center of a motif and working outward; this maintains an even tension, so that the motif lies flat. Fasten your sewing thread on the wrong side, then, proceeding around the circle, work a tiny stitch over a crochet stitch, take the thread underneath the fabric for a short distance (to the next cluster of stitches, for example), and make another tiny stitch; repeat. Pull the thread slightly over the crochet to hide it, but take care not to pull it between stitches, which would cause the work to pucker.

Once you have all your motifs sewn in place, use a water-erasable pen to draw freehand "stems" for your flowers, weaving them in and out of the motifs as shown in the photographs. Using a crochet thread matching the motif at the top of the stem and a crewel or chenille needle, work small running stitches following the lines.

"AMORE" PITCHER COVER

This project has been on my mind for some time. Last summer I made some wineglass tags for a client and used little quartz droplets and coral beads combined with leather string and silver findings. As soon as I saw the quartz drops, I knew they would be perfect for a pitcher cover—I just needed an excuse to make another one. (Oh yes, I already have a couple in the kitchen!) Ever the magpie, I just love a little bit of sparkle. As I sit writing and making this cover the little gems are reflecting the early autumn sunlight and it's bouncing around the kitchen—a sprinkle of natural magic to brighten the soul.

YOU WILL NEED

Anchor Pearl Cotton no. 8, shade 186: 1 x 10 g ball

Crochet hook: 1.25 mm or 7 steel

Crystals and beads: 10 coral-colored beads $\frac{1}{16}$ inch (2 mm) in diameter; 5 pink quartz faceted drops, 5 blue quartz faceted drops (from Gemme Tresor, Etsy), both $\frac{5}{16}$ inch (8 mm) long

Beading needle, size 10–12, for threading

Sewing thread, any color

Tapestry needle

GAUGE

45 dc to 4 inches (10 cm)

FINISHED SIZE

The pitcher cover measures about 5 inches (12.5 cm) in diameter, excluding beads.

LEVEL

Confident It has taken me many attempts to perfect the repeating heart motif used in this design; I hope it will be easier to follow than it was to create!

INSTRUCTIONS

Thread the beads and quartz onto the pearl cotton, starting with blue quartz, then coral bead, pink quartz, coral bead and repeat (see page 26).

Round 1 start with a slip ring. 1 sc and ch 2 into ring (counts as 1 dc), 14 dc into ring, sl st into top of 2 ch.

Round 2 ch 5 (counts as 1 dc, 2 ch), * working into back loop only, 1 dc into next st, ch 2 *, repeat from * to *, sl st into 3rd of 5 ch.

Round 3 sl st into ch space, ch 3 into ch space, 1 dc into same ch space, * ch 2, 2 dc into next ch space *, repeat from * to *, ch 2, sl st into top of 3 ch.

Round 4 ch 1, 1 sc into next dc, * 2 sc into ch space, 1 sc into each of next 2 dc *, repeat from * to *, 2 sc into ch space, sl st into 1 ch.

Round 5 ch 2 (counts as 1 hdc), 1 hdc into each st, sl st into top of 2 ch.

Round 6 ch 4 (counts as 1 tr), 1 tr into next hdc, * ch 4, skip 2 sts, 1 tr into each of next 2 sts *, repeat from * to *, ch 4, skip 2 sts, sl st into top of 4 ch.

Round 7 sl st into next tr, ch 3 (counts as 1 dc), 2 dc into same tr, * ch 4, skip next tr, 3 dc into next tr *, repeat from * to * to form base of hearts, ch 4, sl st into top of 3 ch.

Round 8 ch 3 (counts as 1 dc), 1 dc into each of next 2 dc, 1 dc into next ch, ch 3, skip 2 ch, 1 dc into next ch, 1 dc into each of next 3 dc, 1 dc into next ch, ch 3, skip next 2 ch *, repeat from * to *, 1 dc into last ch, sl st into top of 3 ch.

Round 9 ch 3 (counts as 1 dc), 1 dc into each of next 3 dc, 1 dc into next ch, skip 1 ch, * 1 dc into next ch, 1 dc into each of next 5 dc, 1 dc into next ch, skip 1 ch *, repeat from * to *, 1 dc into next ch, 1 dc into last ch, sl st into top of 3 ch.

Round 10 working into back loop only of each st, sl st into next dc (this forms center of first heart; the other half

of this heart will be at the end of the round), 1 sc into next dc, 2 dc into next dc, 1 sc into next dc, sl st between this dc and first dc of next heart, * 1 sc into first dc of next heart, 2 dc into next dc, 1 sc into next dc, sl st into center dc, 1 sc into next dc, 2 dc into next dc, 1 sc into next dc, sl st between this dc and first dc of next heart *, repeat from * to * to start of first heart, 1 sc into next dc, 2 dc into next dc, 1 sc into last dc, sl st into first sl st.

Round 7 forms the base of the hearts; rounds 8 and 9 form the main body of the hearts; round 10 forms the shaped top of the hearts.

Round 11 slip st into next 2 sts to top of heart shape, * ch 6, sl st into center of right-hand side of next heart, ch

6, sl st into center of opposite side of same heart *, repeat from * to *, ch 6, sl st into center of right-hand side of first heart, ch 6, sl st into same st as original sl st.

Round 12 sl st to center of first ch arch, 1 sc, ch 9, * 1 sc into center of next ch arch, ch 9 *, repeat from * to *, sl st into first sc.

Round 13 repeat round 12.

Round 14 ch 1, * (5 sc into next ch arch, ch 3, sl st into last sc to form picot, 5 sc into same ch arch) twice, 3 sc into next ch arch, ch 1, ch 1 inserting coral bead, ch 1 inserting quartz drop, sl st into 1 ch before coral bead, ch 1, 3 sc into same ch space *, repeat from * to *, finishing with a sl st into first sc. Fasten off.

This is one of my all-time favorite projects. For me, a table set for a special occasion isn't complete without hand-finished linen napkins, and I love to make my own from beautiful slubby linen in a natural color and then edge them with delicate crochet. They also make good presents for friends or family. If you don't want to bother making your own napkins, you can use store-bought ones. The ones I've used here are natural linen embellished with hemstitching. Their open weave makes a good base for crochet. Using cotton yarn to edge your napkins means that you can put them through the wash again and again.

YOU WILL NEED

One or more natural linen napkins, about 18 x 18 inches (45 x 45 cm)

Debbie Bliss Ecobaby Fairtrade Collection, shade 028 Heather: 1 x 50 g (1¾ oz) ball (3 napkins) or 2 balls (for 6)

Crochet hooks: 1.25 mm and 2.25 mm or 7 steel and B / 1 (optional; see Instructions)

Tapestry needle

GAUGE

One triangle measures about ⅝ inches (1.5 cm) wide by ½ inch (1 cm) deep.

FINISHED SIZE

Napkin with edging measures about 18½ x 18½ inches (47 x 47 cm).

LEVEL

Moving on There is nothing complicated about the pattern, but it can be tricky learning to work the single crochet into the napkin edge. Once you've mastered this technique, you'll find yourself edging anything with a straight, plain edge—tablecloths, table runners, hand towels, the hems of little girls' dresses . . .

INSTRUCTIONS

Round 1 Using smaller hook and holding napkin with edge uppermost (away from you), insert hook from front to back about ¼ inch (5 mm) from edge of napkin, hook the yarn and pull it to the right side. (Note that if the hem is more than ¼ inch (5 mm) deep, you will need to work through two layers of fabric. If you find it difficult to work the crochet with such a small hook, use it just to make the holes in the fabric, then use the larger hook for the crochet.) Work 1 long sc (over the hem or over about ¼ inch [5 mm]), then ch 1. Continue along the edge, working 1 long sc and ch 1 alternately, spacing the sc about ¼ inch (5 mm) apart. At each corner work 3 sc, each separated by ch 2. Finish with a sl st into first sc.

Round 2 change to the larger hook (if you have been using the smaller one to crochet round 1). Always working into back loop only of sts of previous round, ch 2, skip 1 st, * 1 sc, 1 hdc, ch 2, 1 hdc, 1 sc into next sc (this will give you a little triangle shape), ch 1, skip 1 st, sl st into next sc, ch 1, skip 1 st *, repeat from * to * across each side. At the corners, work a triangle pattern into the corner st, even if it means skipping the space between the previous triangle and this one. Finish with a sl st into first ch. Fasten off.

LIVING ROOM

At the end of a long day, The Sicilian and
I will often curl up in the living room with
a glass of wine. Whether it's relaxing,
entertaining, or catching up on our
favorite blogs, comfort is key. If you have
a decorating scheme, bring it together with
the art on your walls, the coasters on your
coffee table, and the pillows on your sofa.
Varying shades of complementary colors work
well, as can a variety of textures.

When I joined my local sewing group at Daisy May's in Wareham, one of the first projects I completed was a case for my beloved PowerBook (now in its eighth year and, they say, obsolete; yet here I am tapping away on it). This case can be made to fit all sorts of electronic devices—a laptop or a tablet, such as an iPad or a Kindle; just adjust the size of your case and zipper and make more or fewer motifs. I am always looking for craft projects to do for the men in my life, so I thought I would try to make this as "macho" as possible. I used an Italian thread, ISPE Perlè Ricamo, for the motifs shown, but the threads specified opposite are a good substitute.

YOU WILL NEED

Anchor Pearl Cotton no. 8, shades 341 (brick red), 922 (blue) and 276 (cream): 1 x 10 g ball of each

Crochet hook: 1.00 mm or 11 steel

Tapestry needle

Tobacco-colored linen, at least 36 inches (90 cm) wide: ³⁄₈ yard (30 cm)

Sewing thread to match motifs

Sewing needle

Brown pearl cotton no. 8, slightly darker than fabric: small amount

Crewel or chenille needle

Lightweight polyester batting: ³⁄₈ yard (30 cm)

Spray adhesive

Metal general-purpose zip, 10 inches (25 cm) long

Sewing machine

GAUGE

Gauge is not critical for this project.

FINISHED SIZE

The case measures about 10½ x 8 inches (27 x 20 cm).

LEVEL

Moving on The circular targets are quite simple, but you need to be able to start with a slip ring, working your stitches into it, then pulling it tight. Alternatively, you can make a loop of chains and work into this, but preferably no more than 3 chains to avoid making a big hole in the center of the target.

NOTE

The positions of the targets as stated in the instructions on page 65 are based on the case when held with the zipper on top, not as positioned in the photograph.

INSTRUCTIONS

Small targets B and C to each side of central smallest target

Use colors in order of preference; this pattern will work with the brick red, blue, and then cream for target B (target C is blue, cream, then brick red). Fasten off after each stripe. When beginning a new color, work the first 10–12 stitches over the tail of the new yarn—one less end to sew in.

Round 1 using red for target B (blue for target C) start with a slip ring, 1 sc into ring and ch 2 (counts as 1 dc), 14 dc into ring, sl st into top of 2 ch.

Round 2 change to blue (cream for target C) and join to the top of a dc, ch 4 (counts as 1 tr), 1 tr into same st, 2 tr into each dc, sl st into top of 4 ch (30 sts).

Round 3 attach cream (red for target C) to the top of a tr, ch 5 (counts as 1 dtr), 1 dtr into same st, 2 dtr into each tr, sl st into top of 5 ch (60 sts).

Round 4 continuing with cream (red for target C), ch 1, * 1 sc into each of next 2 sts, 2 sc into following st *, repeat from * to * to end, sl st into 1 ch.

Smallest target D and medium target E

Target D (cream, red, then blue) follows exactly the same pattern as B and C, but on round 3 begin with only ch 4 and substitute tr for dtr. Target E (blue, cream, red, cream) in the top right-hand corner of the case is the same as pattern D to end of round 3.

Round 4 attach cream to the top of a tr, ch 2, 1 hdc into each tr, sl st into top of 2 ch.

Round 5 ch 1, 2 sc into each hdc, sl st in 1 ch.

Large target A in bottom left-hand corner

Start as for small targets to end of round 3 (color cream, brick red, then blue, change back to cream for round 4), but do not cut yarn at the end of round 4.

Round 5 ch 3 (counts as 1 dc), * 2 dc into next st, 1 dc into following st *, repeat from * to * to end, ch 3, sl st into top of 3 ch.

Round 6 using red, ch 4 (counts as 1 tr), 1 tr into each st to end, sl st into top of 4 ch.

To finish

For the cover and lining cut 4 pieces of linen, each 12 x 9 inches (30 x 22.5 cm). From the batting cut 2 pieces, each 10½ x 7½ inches (27 x 19 cm).

Hand-seal the motifs to one of the cover pieces as shown (or in your own preferred arrangement), fastening the center tail of thread to the fabric on the wrong side. Use sewing thread and needle to slipstitch them in place neatly around the edges.

Using spray adhesive, stick the batting to the wrong side of both cover pieces, leaving an even margin of fabric all around. Using the brown pearl cotton and the crewel or chenille needle, work several lines of running stitch through the front cover piece and batting to add some texture and depth.

Press under ½ inch (1 cm) on one long edge of the back cover piece and on the top long edge of the front cover piece. Pin each pressed-under edge alongside the teeth of the (closed) zipper, taking care to center the zipper along the length of the fabric. Baste in place, then topstitch by machine, using the zipper foot. Remove the basting and open the zipper. Turn the two cover pieces so that their right sides are facing and raw edges are aligned. Stitch them together along the remaining three sides, taking ⅜ inch (1 cm) seam allowance. Press seam flat and cut diagonally across lower corners to reduce bulk.

Stitch the two lining pieces together, right sides facing, along one long and both short sides, this time taking ⅝ inch (1.5 cm) seam allowance. Press seam flat, trim to about ¼ inch (5 mm) and cut diagonally across the lower corners. Turn ⅝ inch (1.5 cm) to the wrong side on the top edge of the lining; press. Slip the lining into the cover and push it well down so that the pressed edge lies under the zipper tape and just overlaps the outer cover's seam allowances. Baste the lining in place, then secure it with slipstitches.

Tunisian crochet lends itself to textile work. It produces a thick panel of fabric suitable for garments, throw pillows or, in this case, a crochet hook roll. Initially I planned to make a simple little bag, but frustrated by my existing crochet bag—I can never find the right hook when I need it, searching among scissors, needles, threads and so on—I chose this altogether more ordered approach. I only wish I'd made it before beginning the book, so I could have had all of my hooks beautifully lined up in order of size, ready for anything. I've used a strip of leather as a tie, but you could instead use a length of grosgrain ribbon. As an optional embellishment I've sewn a lacy motif to the lining; you'll find the pattern on page 54 (it is the large purple motif on the table runner).

YOU WILL NEED

Sirdar Snuggly Baby Bamboo DK, shade 163: 2 x 50 g (1¾ oz) balls

Tunisian crochet hook: 3.50 mm or E / 4

Tapestry needle

Linen for lining, at least 36 inches (90 cm) wide: ⅜ yard (30 cm)

Water-erasable pen

Ruler

Piece of leather about 28 inches (70 cm) in length, or grosgrain ribbon, ½ inch (1 cm) wide: ¾ yard (70 cm)

Sewing machine

Sewing thread to match crochet, lining and tie

For motif: any white no. 10 crochet cotton

Crochet hook: 1.25mm or 7 steel

White sewing thead

Sewing needle

GAUGE

25 sts and 23 rows of simple stitch to 4 inches (10 cm), worked with a Tunisian hook

FINISHED SIZE

Opened flat, the roll measures about 10½ x 8 inches (27 x 20 cm).

LEVEL

Starting out Even if Tunisian crochet is a new technique for you, this really is the simplest of stitches. Full instructions for the basic Tunisian simple stitch are given on page 28. The key to maintaining a straight edge is to remember to work a single turning chain before you begin the backward journey, but not before beginning the forward journey.

INSTRUCTIONS

Beginning with a slip knot as usual, ch 47.
Work 61 rows of simple stitch. Remember that 1 "row" consists of both a forward and a backward journey. At the end of each forward journey you should have 47 sts on the hook; at the end of the backward journey you should have just 1. Fasten off the last stitch and sew it into the wrong side of the work using a tapestry needle.

For the motif, follow the instructions for the large purple motif on the table runner on page 54, using no. 10 crochet cotton and a 1.25 mm or 7 steel crochet hook.

To finish
Press the Tunisian crochet using a steam iron and protecting the fabric with a cotton or linen press cloth. Don't worry if the edges curl at this stage; this is quite normal for Tunisian crochet.

From the lining fabric cut 3 panels:
• Panel A, 11¾ x 8¾ inches (29 x 22 cm); this covers the whole inner surface of the crochet;
• Panel B, 11¾ x 4¼ inches (29 x 11 cm); this is to hold the crochet hooks;
• Panel C, 11¾ x 5 inches (29 x 13 cm); this is the flap that covers the tops of the hooks.

If you are adding a motif, sew it to panel B at this point, fastening it at the center with the tail from the motif's center and slipstitching (see page 25) neatly around the edges. (I've positioned my motif so that it disappears into the seam, but you can place yours so that all of it will be visible, if you prefer.)

Turn under and topstitch a ½-inch (1 cm) hem on one long edge and both side edges of panel C and on one long edge of panel B.

Pin panel C on top of the right side of panel A with its hemmed edges underneath, its raw edge aligned with one long edge of A, and ⅜ inch (1 cm) of A extending to each side. Stitch them together along their top edges, taking ½ inch (1 cm) seam allowance. Press the seam flat, then fold the seam allowances to the wrong side along the stitching line and press again.

Pin panel B to the right side of panel A, hemmed edge underneath and raw edges aligned. Stitch them together along their side and bottom edges, again taking ½ inch (1 cm) seam allowance (catching in the motif if positioned there). Press the seam as before, fold it under along the stitching line, and press again.

Using a water-erasable pen and ruler, draw vertical lines on panel B to divide it into 7 pockets, each just under 1½ inches (4 cm) wide. Stitch along the lines, taking care when stitching over the motif.

Pin and baste the lining to the crochet around the side and lower edges. Wind the bobbin with thread matching the crochet and thread the needle to match the lining. Pull back the flap (C) to get it out of the way and topstitch through all layers from one top corner to the other, about ¼ inch (5 mm) from the edge, so as to secure the turned edges of the lining, then topstitch along the remaining edge of the lining to join the crochet across the upper edge.

If you are using a leather tie, cut a strip a scant ½ inch (8–9 mm) wide and 28 inches (70 cm) long. With the crochet roll placed crochet side up and with the flap extended, pin the leather (or ribbon) tie to the right-hand edge, halfway between top and bottom of the crochet, with 8 inches (20 cm) of the tie extending to the right of the pin. Topstitch the tie in place, working back and forth several times to fasten it securely.

FRAMED MOTIF

Ever inspired by vintage crochet, I often look at an example and think it's too gorgeous to put under a vase or plate; it should be on the wall as a piece of art. The motif shown here is based on one I made using some vintage cream-colored thread that I found in a secondhand store. I found that the design worked equally well in this pretty peacock blue.

YOU WILL NEED

Anchor Aida Crochet Cotton no. 10, shade 0850:
1 x 50 g (1¾ oz) ball

Crochet hook: 1.00 mm or 11 steel

Picture frame about 9 x 9 inches (23 x 23 cm)

Piece of backing fabric about 2 inches (5 cm) larger in each direction than the backing board of frame

Tapestry needle

Sewing needle and thread to match motif

Fabric glue

GAUGE

25 sc and 20 rows to 4 inches (10 cm)

FINISHED SIZE

The motif measures 6 inches (15 cm) in diameter.

LEVEL

Confident There is quite a lot going on here, such as crocheting into the back of your work and using a fine thread, but if you're feeling confident, give it a try.

INSTRUCTIONS

Round 1 start with a slip ring. 1 sc into ring and ch 5 (counts as 1 tr and 2 ch), * 1 tr into ring, ch 2 *, repeat from * to * 6 times to form a total of 8 spokes, sl st into 3rd of 5 ch. Pull tail to close ring.

Round 2 1 sc, 3 dc and 1 sc into each 2-ch space (8 petals).

Round 3 working behind petals, sl st into back loop only of sl st in 3rd of 5 ch on round 1, * ch 3, sl st into back loop only of next tr of round 1 *, repeat from * to * 6 times, ch 3, sl st into back loop only of first sl st.

Round 4 1 sc, 5 dc and 1 sc into each 3-ch space.

Round 5 working behind petals, sl st into back loop only of first sl st of round 3, * ch 5, sl st into back loop only of next sl st of round 3 *, repeat from * to * 6 times, ch 5, sl st into back loop only of first sl st.

Round 6 1 sc, 7 dc and 1 sc into each 5-ch space.

Round 7 working behind petals, sl st into back loop only of first sl st of round 5, * ch 10, sl st into back loop only of next sl st of round 5 *, repeat from * to * 6 times, ch 10, sl st into back loop only of first sl st.

Round 8 1 sc, 2 hdc, 3 dc, 1 dc, 3 tr, 2 hdc and 1 sc into each 10-ch space.

Round 9 sl st into each of first 6 sts of first petal, * 1 sc into back loop only of tr at center of petal, ch 16 *, repeat from * to * 7 times, sl st into first sc.

Round 10 1 sc, 2 hdc, 7 dc, 1 tr, 7 dc, 2 hdc and 1 sc into each 16-ch space.

Round 11 sl st into each of first 10 sts of first petal, * 1 sc into next tr, ch 24 *, repeat from * to * 7 times, sl st into first sc.

Round 12 1 sc, 2 hdc, 3 dc, 4 tr, 4 dtr, ch 2, 4 dtr, 4 tr, 3 dc, 2 hdc and 1 sc into each 24-ch space, sl st into first sc.

Round 13 * 1 sc into each of first 14 sts of petal, 2 sc, ch 3, sl st into first of ch and 1 sc all into 2-ch space, 1 sc into each of remaining 14 sts of petal *, repeat from * to * 7 times, sl st into first sc. Fasten off.

To finish

Position the motif on the backing fabric (placed on an ironing board) and pin it in place at several points, in the center and around the edge, sticking pins through the ironing board cover to hold everything taut. Thread the sewing needle with matching thread and—removing each pin in turn so you can lift the fabric slightly—use a few tiny stitches to attach the crochet to the fabric. Leave about 6 inches (15 cm) thread ends at start and finish each time, then take both threads to the wrong side and fasten off neatly. Place the fabric wrong side up on a clean, smooth surface and lay the backing board, centered, on top. Using fabric glue, stick the raw edges of the fabric to the board. Allow glue to dry, then assemble the frame.

PROJECT...

COASTERS

Another project inspired by a vintage, thrift shop purchase, these delicate coasters are intended for wine or water glasses, but they could equally take a hot cup of tea. I used an Italian crochet cotton (BBB Ciak 16 Filo di Scozia) for the coaster shown, but I've suggested an equivalent. If you would like something more substantial, use a sport-weight or DK yarn, rather than fine cotton (although this would be too bulky for a wineglass). In that case you would need to reduce the number of rounds accordingly.

YOU WILL NEED

Anchor Artiste Mercer Crochet thread no. 20, shade 386: 1 x 20 g ball is enough to make 6 coasters

Crochet hook: 1.25 mm or 7 steel

Tapestry needle

GAUGE

50 sc and 50 rows to 4 inches (10 cm)

FINISHED SIZE

The coaster measures 3½ inches (9 cm) in diameter.

LEVEL

Moving on This is a super-simple pattern, but it may be best to give it a whirl only once you feel comfortable working with fine cotton yarn.

INSTRUCTIONS

Round 1 start with a slip ring, ch 3 (counts as 1 dc), 13 dc into ring; pull end to close ring, sl st into top of 3 ch. Insert a contrasting marker at this point and move marker up at end of each round.
Round 2 * 2 sc into next st, 1 sc into following st *, repeat from * to * to end.
Round 3 as round 2.
Round 4 * 2 sc into next st, 1 sc into each of following 2 sts *, repeat from * to * to end.
Round 5 * 2 sc into next st, 1 sc into each of following 6 sts *, repeat from * to * to end.
Round 6 1 sc into each st to end.
Round 7 2 sc into next st, 1 sc into each of following 3 sts, * 2 sc into next st, 1 sc into each of following 6 sts *, repeat from * to * to end.
Round 8 2 sc into next st, 1 sc into each of following 4 sts, * 2 sc into next st, 1 sc into each of following 8 sts *, repeat from * to * to end.
Rounds 9–12 * 2 sc into next st, 1 sc into each of following 8 sts *, repeat from * to * to end. Do not stop the pattern and start again at the marker, just keep working.
Round 13 1 sc into each st to end.

Round 14 1 sc into each of next 3 sts, 2 sc into next st, * 1 sc into each of next 10 sts, 2 sc into next st *, repeat from * to * to end.
Round 15 1 sc into each st to end, sl st into first st.
Round 16 * ch 3, skip 1 st, 1 sc into next st *, repeat from * to * ending ch 3, sl st into base of first 3 ch.
Round 17 1 sl st into first ch space, 1 sc, * ch 4, 1 sc into next ch space *, repeat from * to * ending ch 4, sl st into first sc.
Round 18 2 sl st into ch space, 1 sc, repeat round 17 from * to *, ending ch 4, sl st into first sc.
Round 19 as round 18 but with ch 5 between each sc.
Round 20 as round 18 (reverting back to ch 4).
Fasten off.

Last winter I went mad crocheting scarves for all the girls in my life—my daughter, the daughters of friends, sisters-in-law . . . the list goes on. I found myself with an assortment of silk and kid mohair-silk yarn, just waiting to be used up in another project. Living near the coast, I am constantly inspired by our surroundings, and given the array of blues I had accumulated, it seemed natural to bring them together with this wave pattern pillow. The intention is to crochet a panel long enough to cover the front and then wrap around one end of the pillow.

YOU WILL NEED

Rowan Kidsilk Haze, Color A, shade 644 Ember; Color B, shade 592 Heavenly; Color C, shade 642 Ghost; Color D, shade 634 Cream: 1 x 25 g (1 oz) ball of each

Crochet hook: 4 mm or G / 6

Pillow form: 18 x 14 inches (46 x 36 cm); see Note below

Piece of firm linen or cotton fabric, 40 x 14½ inches (102 x 37 cm)

Tapestry needle

Sewing needle

Sewing thread to match fabric plus one contrasting color for basting

Sewing machine

GAUGE

19 sts and 12 rows measure 4 inches (10 cm) over pattern.

FINISHED SIZE

The crochet panel measures 25½ inches (65 cm) long and 13½ inches (34 cm) wide.

LEVEL

Confident This kid mohair-silk blend yarn is beautiful to work with; it glides through your hand. However, it is almost impossible to undo (the fibers fuse together). If you make a mistake, don't worry—the fluffiness is very good at hiding minor errors. (You'd just go crazy trying to work backward.)

NOTE

If you cannot find a pillow form of this size, you can make one, using unbleached muslin and about 1 pound (450 g) polyester fiberfill. Cut a piece of fabric measuring 30 x 19½ inches (76 x 50 cm). Fold it in half across the shorter measurement and stitch it together, taking ¾ inch (2 cm) seam allowance and leaving a gap of about 6 inches (15 cm) in the middle. Turn the work right side out and stuff it with fiberfill, working the stuffing into the corners. Slipstitch (see page 25) the opening edges together.

INSTRUCTIONS

Wind each ball into 2 equal-sized balls. The pattern is worked using two strands together, and it is much easier to get everything ready in advance. Each time you change yarn, leave enough to sew into the panel at the end.

Using 2 strands of Color A ch 67.
Row 1 (right side) skip 1 ch, * 1 sc into each of next 3 ch, 1 hdc into next ch, 1 dc into each of next 3 ch, 1 tr into each of next 3 ch, 1 dc into each of next 3 ch, 1 hdc into next ch *, repeat from * to * 3 times, 1 sc into each of next 3 ch, 1 hdc into next ch, 1 dc into each of next 3 ch, 1 tr into each of last 3 ch, turn.
Row 2 using 1 strand of A and 1 strand of B, ch 1, 1 sc into the back loop only of each st to end, turn.
Row 3 using 2 strands of B, ch 4, skip st at base of ch, working into front loop only of each st, 1 tr into each of next 2 sts, * 1 dc into each of next 3 sts, 1 hdc into next st, 1 sc into each of next 3 sts, 1 hdc into next st, 1 dc into each of next 3 sts, 1 tr into each of next 3 sts *, repeat from * to * 3 times, 1 dc into each of next 3 sts, 1 hdc into next st, 1 sc into each of last 3 sts, turn.
Row 4 using 1 strand of B and 1 strand of C, repeat row 2.
Row 5 using 2 strands of C, ch 1, working into front loop only of each st, * 1 sc into each of next 3 sts, 1 hdc into next st, 1 dc into each of next 3 sts, 1 tr into each of next 3 sts, 1 dc into each of next 3 sts, 1 hdc into next st *, repeat from * to * 3 times, 1 sc into each of next 3 sts, 1 hdc into next st, 1 dc into each of next 3 sts, 1 tr into each of last 3 sts, turn.
Row 6 using 1 strand of C and 1 strand of D, repeat row 2.
Row 7 using 2 strands of D, repeat row 3.
Row 8 using 1 strand of D and 1 strand of A, repeat row 2.
Row 9 using 2 strands of A, repeat row 5.
Repeat rows 2–9 eight times, then work rows 2–7 again.
Fasten off.

To finish
Begin by machine-stitching a ¾-inch (2-cm) hem in both of the shorter ends of the fabric. Now mark off the front section of the cover by gently pressing a fold 8 inches (20 cm) from one hemmed edge and another fold 17¾ inches (45 cm) away from the first fold. The remaining section of fabric should measure about 12½ inches (32 cm). This will allow ends to overlap by about 2¾ inches (7 cm).

Place the crocheted panel on the cover with the wavy edge (final row worked) slightly overlapping the hem at the start of the shortest section and the first row worked level with the second fold. Baste it in place around the edges, using contrasting thread for easy removal later and making sure that the panel's side edges lie less than ½ inch (1 cm) from the fabric edges, so that they will be secured in the seam.

Now bring the two end sections over the center section, enclosing it, with the smaller end underneath the larger end section. (The wrong sides of these sections are now uppermost; when the cover is turned right side out, the smaller section will overlap the larger one.) Pin and baste the cover together along the raw edges, catching in the crochet. Stitch, taking ½ inch (1 cm) seam allowance (or a little more, if your panel barely fits the width—pillow forms will squeeze in a little if necessary).

Turn the cover right side out, remove the basting, and insert the pillow form.

BEDROOM

To me a bedroom is more than just a space
to sleep in. It is a sanctuary away from
the hectic pace of daily life. Very much
inspired by the coast, I have injected a
bit of seaside color here, with corals
and turquoise. And a bedroom is the
perfect place for a little luxury—hence
the cashmere slippers and lace-trimmed
Liberty print panties!

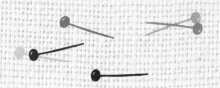

I just love linen—the way it washes, the way it creases, and the feel of it against my face. It made perfect sense to introduce some brighter shades into the bedroom, and when I found these linens I had no more excuses. Linen is also ideal for trimming with crochet, because you can so easily pass your crochet hook between the warp and weft threads; if you are gentle, they part naturally and there is no need to punch holes in the fabric. If you prefer to use a pretty, closely woven cotton, use a smaller hook to make the holes first. Or use a crewel or chenille needle to edge the pillowcase with chain stitch, making the stitches relatively short and fat (work a sample first to determine the best spacing), then work your crochet stitches into this foundation.

YOU WILL NEED

Two linen pillowcases with envelope closures (on underside of case), or plain pillowcases

Red edging: Rowan Siena, shade 668 Beacon: 1 x 50 g (1¾ oz) ball

Gray edging: DMC Natura Just Cotton, shade 3 Sable (sand): 1 x 50 g (1¾ oz) ball

Crochet hooks: 2.25 mm and 1.25 mm or B / 1 and 7 steel

Tapestry needle

2 yards (2 m) satin ribbon to match pillowcase (optional)

Sewing needle and thread to match ribbon (optional)

Crewel or chenille needle (optional)

GAUGE

Both edgings: 29 sts of sc to 4 inches (10 cm)

FINISHED SIZE

Both edgings measure about ¾ inch (2 cm) in depth.

LEVEL

Moving on You need to get used to the long single crochet required to edge the pillowcase, and you need to be able to adapt your pattern slightly on the last few stitches if it doesn't quite fit perfectly around your pillowcase. It is important to start at the back of your pillowcase; that way, if you need to skip a stitch to finish or add in an extra half pattern repeat, it will be out of sight.

SPECIAL INSTRUCTION

Partial sc Work the first part of your sc by hooking the yarn through your next stitch or chain space (2 loops on hook), then do the same into the next stitch or chain space (3 loops on hook), then finish both sc together by hooking yarn and bringing it back through all 3 loops at once. Also known as 2 sc together (2 sc tog).

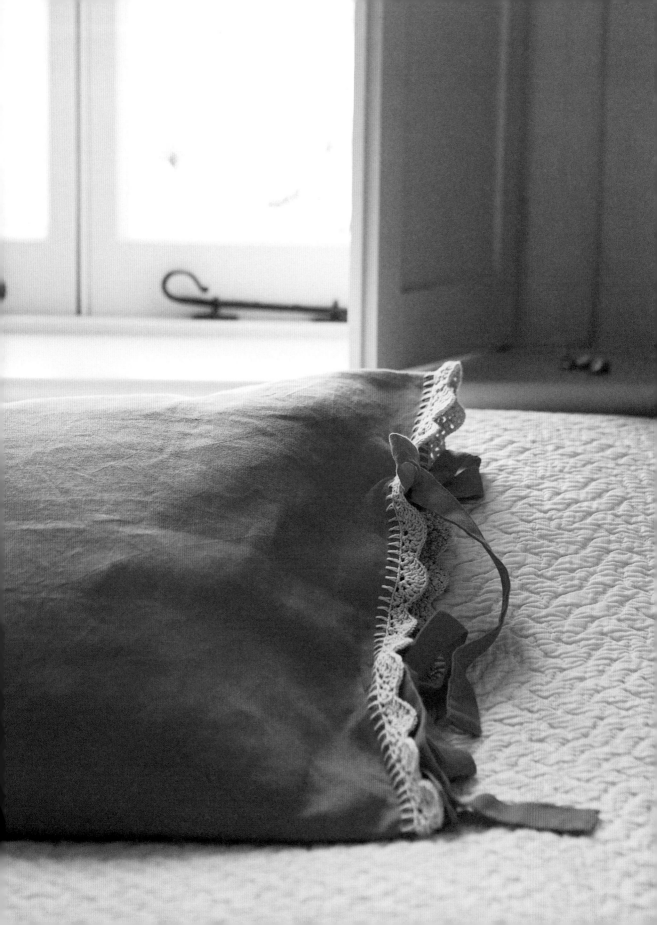

INSTRUCTIONS

Red edging

If you are using a flap-type pillowcase you will need to press a sharp crease along the place where the back becomes the flap. The edging is worked through this folded thickness of fabric and (on the front) through the hemmed edge. If you are using an ordinary pillowcase you can simply work through the opening edge all the way around.

Round 1 using smaller hook and holding pillowcase with edge uppermost (away from you), insert hook from front to back about ½ inch (1 cm) from edge of pillowcase, hook the yarn and pull it to the right side. (Note: if you find it difficult to work the crochet with such a small hook, use it just to make the holes in the fabric, then use the larger hook for the crochet.) Work 1 long sc over about ½ inch (1 cm), then ch 2. Continue around the edge working 1 long sc and ch 2 alternately, spacing the sc about ½ inch (1 cm) apart. Finish with a sl st into first sc.

Round 2 change to larger hook, ch 3, skip 1 st, 1 sc into next st *, ch 2, skip 1 st, 1 sc into next st *, repeat from * to *, ending ch 2, skip 1 st, sl st into first of 3 ch.

Round 3 1 sc into next ch space, ch 2, partial sc (see page 80) in same ch space, partial sc into next ch space, yarn over and pull through all 3 loops (makes 2 sc together, or 2 sc tog), * 2 sc tog into same and next ch space *, repeat from * to *, ending 2 ch, partial sc into same ch space, sl st into top of first sc, pulling through both loops on hook.

Rounds 4 and 5 repeat round 3. Fasten off.

Gray edging

Work round 1 as for red edging using gray yarn.

Round 2 change to larger hook. ch 4, sl st into top of next sc (skip the ch in between), * ch 4, sl st into top of next sc *, repeat from * to *, ending sl st into first of 4 ch.

Round 3 sl st into first and 2nd ch, ch 2, * (1 dc, ch 1, 1 dc, ch 1, 1 dc, ch 1 and 1 dc) into next ch space, ch 1, 1 sc into next ch space, ch 2, 1 sc into next ch space, ch 3, 1 sc into next ch space, ch 2, 1 sc into next ch space, ch 1 *, repeat from * to *, ending sl st into first of 2 ch.

Round 4 1 sc into ch space, ch 2, 1 dc into same space, ch 1, 2 dc and ch 1 into each of next 4-ch spaces, * skip 1-ch space, 1 sc into next ch sp, ch 1, skip 1-ch space, 2 dc and ch 1 into each of next 5-ch spaces *, repeat from * to * to end, sl st into first sc. Fasten off.

Ribbon Ties

For the optional ties, simply cut the ribbon into 4 lengths, press under about ¼ inch (5 mm) on one short end, and hand-sew this end along the inner side of the edging, positioning two ties opposite each other as shown.

BOOKMARK

As well as getting inspiration from my beautiful surroundings, I also get excited by the profusion of crochet on the worldwide Web. One of my favorite blogs is that of the hugely talented Cornel Strydom. Based in South Africa, she writes regularly on her "i love pom-poms" blog. She cleverly selects the best handiwork of the crochet community, whether it be from an individual, from a member of her local group of craft enthusiasts, her own work, or something seen on the Paris catwalk. Not long ago she flagged up the Martha Stewart "granny square" page, upon which was a special little granny square bookmark. I instantly fell in love with it and made several. With my own design, I wanted to incorporate a little sunburst into each square, so here we are. It is made in the finest cotton I have ever tried to use, but be patient: the finished result is gorgeous. It makes a perfect present for a friend who loves books.

YOU WILL NEED

Color A (turquoise): Anchor Artiste Mercer Cotton, no. 80, shade 0250: 1 x 5 g ball

Color B (coral): Anchor Artiste Mercer Cotton, no. 80, shade 0328: 1 x 5 g ball

Color C (teal blue): Anchor Pearl Cotton, no. 8, shade 0168: 1 x 10g ball

Color D (eau de nil): Anchor Artiste Mercer Cotton, no. 20, shade 1042: 1 x 20g ball

Crochet hooks: 1.00 mm and 0.75 mm or 11 and 12 steel

Small sewing needle

GAUGE

Each square measures ⅞ inch (2.2 cm).

FINISHED SIZE

Bookmark measures 7½ x 1⅛ inches (19 x 3 cm).

LEVEL

Confident The pattern is not complicated, but working with such fine yarn comes with its own challenges. Make sure to work in good light and give the work your whole attention.

NOTE

Use the smaller hook for Colors A and B, the larger hook for Colors C and D.

INSTRUCTIONS

Round 1 using color A and smaller hook, make a slip ring, 1 sc and ch 3 into ring (counts as 1 dc), 15 dc into ring, sl st into top of 3 ch.

Round 2 change to color B, ch 4 (counts as 1 tr), 1 tr into same st, 2 tr into each dc, sl st into top of 4 ch (32 sts).

Round 3 using larger hook attach color C, ch 1, working into back loop only of each st, 1 sc into each st, sl st into 1 ch.

Round 4 attach color D, ch 1, working into back loop only

of each st, 1 sc into each of first 5 sts, 1 dc into next st, * 1 dc, ch 2 and 1 dc into next st—corner, 1 dc into next st, 1 sc into each of next 5 sts, 1 dc into next st *, repeat from * to * twice, 1 dc, ch 2 and 1 dc into next st, 1 dc into last st, sl st into 1 ch. Fasten off.

Make 3 more squares in the same way.

Make 4 squares using Color B for round 1 and Color A for round 2.

To finish

Place the squares in alternating order, as shown. Pick up two adjacent squares and place them together with wrong sides facing. Using color C and larger hook, work a row of sc through inner loops of the two adjacent edges. Join the remaining squares in the same way.

Using color C and larger hook, join the yarn to one corner ch space of bookmark.

Round 1 ch 1, * 2 sc, ch 1 and 2 sc into corner, 1 sc into each st to next corner *, repeat from * to * 3 times, sl st into 1 ch.

Round 2 ch 1, working into back loop only of each st, * 1 sc into each st to next corner ch space, 1 sc, ch 1 and 1 sc into corner ch space, * repeat from * to * 3 times, 1 sc into each sc to end, sl st into 1 ch. Fasten off.

This is one of those simple projects that make a very welcome gift for a girlfriend or relative (or even yourself) in need of some warm toes. I've used cashmere for extra luxury, but any DK yarn would be suitable. I've decorated the slippers with embroidered flowers, but you could instead sew on a few buttons.

YOU WILL NEED

Rowan Pure Cashmere DK, shade 823 Greige: 2 x 25 g (1 oz) balls

Small amounts of pink, white, and charcoal gray DK yarn for edging and embroidered flowers

Crochet hook: 3.5 mm or E / 4

Tapestry needle

GAUGE

22 sts and 24 rows of sc to 4 inches (10 cm)

FINISHED SIZE

This pattern is for a size 8 foot (European 39–40, U.K. 6–7); to adapt it for a smaller/larger foot, simply remove/add 2 rows per size from the middle section of the pattern.

LEVEL

Moving on The slippers are worked mainly in simple single crochet, though the shaping requires some concentration.

NOTE

The right and left slippers are identical, apart from the positioning of the decorations.

INSTRUCTIONS

Ch 10.

Round 1 (this starts the toe section) 1 sc into 2nd ch from hook, 1 sc into each of next 7 ch, 3 sc into last ch, working into other side of ch work 1 sc into each of next 7 ch, 2 sc into same ch as first sc, sl st into back loop only of first sc (20 sts).

Round 2 1 sc into each of first 8 sc, 2 sc into each of next 3 sc, 1 sc into each of next 7 sc, 2 sc into each of next 2 sc, 1 sc into same place as first sc, sl st into back loop only of first sc (26 sts).

Round 3 *1 sc into each of first 9 sc, 1 sc and 1 hdc into next st, 1 hdc and 1 dc into next st, 1 dc and 1 hdc into next st, 1 hdc into next st *, repeat from * to * once, sl st into back loop only of first sc (34 sts).

Round 4 1 sc into each of first 11 sts, 2 hdc into each of next 4 sts, 1 sc into each of next 13 sts, 2 hdc into each of next 4 sts, 1 sc into each of last 2 sts, sl st into back loop only of first sc (42 sts).

Round 5 1 sc into each st, sl st into back loop only of first sc.

Rounds 6–21 repeat round 5.

Round 22 sl st into each of first 9 sts for instep, 1 sc into each of 33 sts, turn.

Work forward and backward in rows on these 33 sts for sides and sole.

Row 1 ch 1, skip first sc, 1 sc into each sc to end, turn.

Rows 2–4 repeat row 1 (29 sts).

Rows 5–32 ch 1, 1 sc into each sc to end, turn.

Rows 33 sl st into each of first 9 sts, 1 sc into each of next 11 sts, turn.

Work on these 11 sts for heel.

Rows 34–43 repeat row 1. Fasten off.

To finish

Sew the 9 sts at each end of row 33 to row-ends of heel. Using the same yarn, attach it to the back of your slipper and work around of sc around the top edge, spacing sts evenly. Using a contrasting yarn, work 1 sc into each st of previous round. Fasten off.

Add embroidered flowers, as shown, if desired, using a tapestry needle and contrasting yarn. For petals, work 5 or 6 lazy daisy stitches: bring needle up at inner point of petal, form yarn into small loop, anchor loop at outer point of petal with a tiny straight stitch. Work a few straight stitches in a different color to represent flower centers. Alternatively, decorate the slipper by sewing on a few buttons.

These really are just a bit of fun. I actually made the panties myself, using my beloved Tana Lawn, but the edging can be attached to any store-bought panties you like—or maybe to a slip or camisole or nightgown. If you're sewing the lace to an elasticized edge, make sure to stretch the elastic as you stitch; the lace needs to expand as you put the panties on.

YOU WILL NEED

Anchor Artiste Mercer Crochet thread no. 20, shade 893: 1 x 20 g ball

Crochet hook: 1.25 mm or 7 steel

Tapestry needle

Store-bought panties

Sewing machine

Matching sewing thread

GAUGE

50 hdc to 4 inches (10 cm)

FINISHED SIZE

The edging measures about 32 inches (81 cm) in length.

LEVEL

Moving on This is another simple pattern, but working with fine thread and a small hook can be taxing. Make sure you've got good light and a chair that supports your back well.

INSTRUCTIONS

Make 213 ch.
Foundation row (right side) skip first ch, work 1 sc into each ch, turn.
Row 2 * ch 1, skip 1 st, 1 hdc into next st, ch 1, work 2 hdc around stem of hdc *, repeat from * to * to end of row. Fasten off.

Make another strip of lace for other leg of panties.

To apply
Place the straight edge of the lace just over the edge of one panty leg opening and topstitch it in place, stretching the fabric, if elasticized, as you go. If you find that the the lace is too long, fold the end under as you finish stitching it on, pulling the excess (as much as possible) clear of the stitching line. Then lift the presser foot, turn the work 90 degrees, and stitch through both ends of lace several times, using zigzag stitch, to prevent the lace

from unraveling. Then cut away the excess. Under no circumstances cut the lace before you have secured it in this way. If the two ends of the crochet meet with no overlap, there is no need to stitch them together.

BATHROOM

The bathroom in our cottage is a little
cold and rather damp, but then this is an
old cottage in the woods. Despite my
best efforts at brightening it up—such as a
token vintage bamboo mirror—it clearly
needed an injection of color, and that was my
inspiration for the projects here. Choose your
colors to suit your existing scheme. If,
like mine, your bathroom is a blend of off-
whites, why not hit it with some gorgeous
pastels? Then, come spring and summer,
you can enhance the effect by filling the
bud vases with bunches of pastel-colored,
beautifully scented blooms. Heavenly.

A very simple project, but lovely for bringing a bit of extra color into a bathroom. I've used a variety of yarns for these two "His" and "Hers" washcloths in order to get the right shades, but all of them have a high cotton content, so are washable, durable, and great exfoliators. If you wish to hang your washcloths on hooks, simply work a loop of about a dozen chains on one corner as you are edging the washcloth. The same pattern could be used to make dishcloths; just substitute a dishcloth cotton for the more expensive yarns used here.

YOU WILL NEED

For "His" washcloth

Color A: Debbie Bliss Bella, shade 014 Duck Egg: 1 x 50 g (1¾ oz) ball

Color B: Debbie Bliss Bella, shade 015 Sea Green: 1 x 50 g (1¾ oz) ball

Color C: DMC Natura Just Cotton, shade Sable: 1 x 50 g (1¾ oz) ball

For "Her" washcloth

Color A: Debbie Bliss Ecobaby, shade 028 Heather: 1 x 50 g (1¾ oz) ball

Color B: Rowan Fine Milk Cotton, shade 501 Sepia: 1 x 50 g (1¾ oz) ball

Color C: DMC Natura Just Cotton, shade Sable (use same ball as for edging "His" washcloth).

For both washcloths

Crochet hook: 3.25 mm or D / 3

Tapestry needle

GAUGE

Gauge is not critical on this project.

FINISHED SIZE

Each washcloth measures about 9 x 9 inches (23 x 23 cm).

LEVEL

Starting out This is a great project for developing an even tension and keeping the side edges straight.

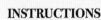

INSTRUCTIONS

"His" washcloth

Using color A, make 51 ch.

Foundation row 1 sc into 2nd from hook, 1 sc into each ch to end, turn.

Rows 1–32 ch 1, 1 sc into each sc to end, turn.

Rows 33–52 cut off color A; attach color B, and continue working 1 sc into each st, again working ch 1 at the beginning of each row. Fasten off.

Edging attach color C to first st of last row, ch 1, 2 sc into this first corner, then work 1 sc into each st across the top edge, 3 sc into corner stitch, 1 sc into the center of each stitch along the side; work into the bottom and remaining side edge as for the first two edges, sl st into first sc. Fasten off.

"Her" washcloth

Follow the same pattern as for "His" washcloth. However, because the yarn I have selected is finer, work 36 rows in color A, followed by 20 rows in color B. Edge the washcloth as given for "His" version.

These linen hand towels remind me of the gorgeous vintage ones my friend Jenny hangs in her bathroom. They haven't got the absorbency of those made from terry cloth, but they dry out quickly and feel crisp and fresh. In my little tribute to The Sicilian, who pressed the hems for me, the words "water", "soap" and "linen" are written here in Italian: Acqua, Sapone, and Lino. The writing is made simply of a length of chains, and the optional motifs I've sewn on are drawn from other projects. The yarns used for the writing were left over from the Bathroom Storage Vessels (pages 96–9); one 50 g (1¾ oz) ball was enough for the bowl and the matching towel.

YOU WILL NEED

For Sapone towel

Debbie Bliss Ecobaby Fairtrade Collection, shade 028 Heather: 1 x 50 g (1¾ oz) ball

For motif (see smaller green flower, page 124): Anchor Artiste Mercer Crochet thread, no. 20, shade 1042: 1 x 20 g ball

For Lino towel

Debbie Bliss Eco Fairtrade Collection, shade 603 Gold: 1 x 50 g (1¾ oz) ball.

For motif (see turquoise flower, pages 124–5): Anchor Artiste Mercer Crochet thread no. 20, shade 968: 1 x 20 g ball

For Acqua towel

Debbie Bliss Bella, shade 015 Sea Green: 1 x 50 g (1¾ oz) ball

For motif (see pink motif, page 129): Anchor Artiste Linen Crochet thread no. 10, shade 392: 1 x 50 g (1¾ oz) ball

For all three towels

Piece of medium- to heavyweight linen: ⅞ yard (80 cm) of fabric at least 51 inches (130 cm) wide, such as Zweigart Cork (55 inches [140 cm]) wide; or three linen hand towels

Crochet hook: 2.25 mm or B / 1 (for writing; for motifs, see relevant projects)

Water-erasable marker

Ruler

Sewing machine

Sewing thread to match yarns and linen

Tapestry needle

GAUGE

14 ch to 2 inches (5 cm)

FINISHED SIZE

Towels shown measure about 24 x 16 inches (60 x 40 cm).

LEVEL

Starting out The ultimate in beginners' projects: all you need to do is work a length of chains and sew it on. The towels would look great with just the words.

INSTRUCTIONS

If you are making your own towels, cut the linen to the size given above (or your preferred size) plus hem allowances of ½ inch (1 cm). Press under ¼ inch (5 mm) twice on side edges; machine stitch. Repeat on top and bottom edges. Using the water-erasable marker, draw guidelines on your towel at the height you want your letters to be; sizes for the words shown are

given below. Then write your choice of words in between the guidelines.

Acqua towel

The word measures 8¼ inches (21 cm) long; the capital "A," 3¼ inches (8 cm) tall; the lower-case letters, 1¾ inches (4.5 cm) tall. Using the green yarn, ch 255 (you

may need more or fewer to write the word, so do not fasten off yet). Pin the chain to the towel over the marked writing, adjusting the length if necessary, then baste it in place using contrasting thread. Using thread to match the chain in the machine needle and thread to match the linen in the bobbin, machine-stitch the chain to the towel. Work a short length of chain (about 6 ch) to make the crossbar of the "A," and stitch it in place.

Lino towel

This word measures 6¾ inches (17 cm) in length; the capital and lower-case letters measure the same as for Acqua. Using the gold yarn, ch 135. Machine-stitch it in place as described above, first adjusting the length if

necessary. For the dot of the "i," draw a little circle and work straight stitches radiating out from the center to fill it.

Sapone towel

This word measures 9½ inches (24 cm) in length. The capital and lower-case letters are the same as for Acqua. Using the heather yarn, ch 358. Machine-stitch it in place as described above, first adjusting the length if necessary.

To finish

Make optional motifs and hand-sew them to the towel, using thread to match the towel and pulling it down between the crochet stitches to conceal it.

Crochet is extremely versatile, which is one of the aspects that appealed to the decorator in me. If I am not able to find a jar or bowl to suit a decorating scheme, I can just crochet one. These little vessels are lined with scraps of cotton from other projects, but if you prefer to avoid sewing, you could just leave them unlined or maybe embellish them with some crocheted flowers in a contrasting yarn. I have used them in my bathroom, but they would make great desk or dressing table containers too. Even better, if Violet, the cat, or one of the kids knocks one over it doesn't break! Indestructible storage, I love it!

YOU WILL NEED

For pink bowl

Debbie Bliss Ecobaby Fair Trade Collection', shade 028 Heather: 1 x 50 g (1¾ oz) ball

Piece of printed cotton at least 7 x 7 inches (18 x 18 cm), such as Tana Lawn "Eloise" (shown) (optional)

For flower motif inside bowl (optional): 2.25 mm or B / 1 crochet hook

For blue pot

Debbie Bliss Bella, shade 015 Sea Green: 1 x 50 g (1¾ oz) ball

Piece of printed cotton at least 12 x 5½ inches (30 x 14 cm), such as Tana Lawn "Betsy D" (shown) (optional)

For yellow bowl

Debbie Bliss Eco Fair Trade Collection, shade 603 Gold: 1 x 50 g (1¾ oz) ball

Piece of printed cotton at least 17½ x 3½ inches (44 x 9 cm), such as Tilda cotton (shown) (optional)

For all three vessels

Debbie Bliss Baby Cashmerino, shade 100 White: 1 x 50 g (1¾ oz) ball

Crochet hook: 3.5 mm or E / 4

Tapestry needle

Sewing machine or sewing needle (for optional lining)

Matching sewing thread (for optional lining)

GAUGE

21 sc and 20 rows to 4 inches (10 cm)

FINISHED SIZE

Pink bowl: about 2 inches (5 cm) tall and 4¼ inches (11 cm) in diameter

Blue pot: about 4 inches (10 cm) tall and 3½ inches (9 cm) in diameter

Yellow bowl: about 2¾ inches (7 cm) tall and 4¼ inches (11 cm) in diameter

LEVEL

Starting out The basic working method of these is the same as for the apple cozy; so if you crack one, the other should seem even easier.

NOTE

For all three vessels, insert a contrasting marker (about 1½ inches [3 cm] of yarn) between the last stitch of the first round and the first one of the next); this will allow you to see when you have completed a round and eliminates the need to count stitches. Move the marker up at the end of every round.

INSTRUCTIONS

Pink bowl

Worked with the wrong side facing.

Round 1 start with a slip ring, ch 1, 11 sc into ring, sl st into 1 ch, pull thread end to close ring.

Round 2 (insert marker) 2 sc into each st to marker.

Round 3 1 sc into each sc to marker.

Round 4 * 1 sc into next st, 2 sc into following st *, repeat from * to * to marker.

Round 5 as round 3.

Round 6 * 1 sc into each of next 2 sts, 2 sc into following st *, repeat from * to * to marker.

Rounds 7 and 8 as round 3.

Round 9 * 1 sc into each of next 3 sts, 2 sc into following st *, repeat from * to * to marker.

Rounds 10 and 11 as round 3.

Round 12 * 1 sc into each of next 4 sts, 2 sc into following st *, repeat from * to * to marker.

Rounds 13–15 as round 3.

Round 16 * 1 sc into each of next 5 sts, 2 sc into following st *, repeat from * to * to marker.

Rounds 17 and 18 as round 3.

Round 19 1 sc into each st, sl st in last st. Fasten off. Turn right side out.

Round 20 with right side facing, attach contrasting yarn to top edge, ch 1, 1 sc into each st, sl st into 1 ch. Fasten off.

For crocheted flower (optional)

Use same yarn as for bowl and 2.25 mm or B / 1 hook.

Round 1 start with a slip ring, 10 sc into slip ring, pull tight, sl st into first sc.

Round 2 (to form each petal) * working into back loop of each st only, 1 sc, 3 dc and 1 sc into next st, sl st into following st *, repeat from * to * 4 times to form a total of 5 petals. Fasten off.

For lining

Fold the fabric into quarters and trim away the corners in a curve (marking first, if you like) to make a circle about 6¾ inches (17 cm) in diameter. Cut a wedge out of the circle (just less than one quarter) and sew the two edges together with right sides facing, taking about ½ inch (1 cm) seam allowance. Attach the flower (if using) to the bottom of the lining by taking the tail end to the wrong side and fastening it with a few stitches. Insert the lining into the bowl, turn under the raw edge to fit, and slipstitch (see page 25) to the crochet just below the contrasting edging.

Blue pot

Worked with wrong side facing.

Round 1 start with a slip ring, 10 sc into ring, sl st into 1 ch, pull thread end to close ring.

Round 2 (insert marker) 2 sc into each st to marker.

Round 3 1 sc into each st to marker.

Round 4 * 1 sc into next st, 2 sc into following st *, repeat from * to * to marker.

Round 5 * 1 sc into each of next 2 sts, 2 sc into following st *, repeat from * to * to marker. (These first 5 rounds form the base of the pot; the following rounds will build the sides.)

Rounds 6 and 7 1 hdc into each st to marker.

Round 8 * 1 hdc into each of next 4 sts, 2 hdc into following st *, repeat from * to * to marker.

Round 9 * 1 hdc into each of next 7 sts, 2 hdc into following st *, repeat from * to * to marker.

Rounds 10–18 1 hdc into each st.

Round 19 * 1 hdc into each of next 8 sts, 2 hdc into following st *, repeat from * to * to marker.

Rounds 20 and 21 1 sc into each st.

Round 22 * 1 sc into each of next 9 sts, 2 sc into following st *, repeat from * to * to marker. Fasten off. Turn pot right side out.

Round 23 with right side facing, attach contrasting yarn to top edge, ch 1, 1 sc into each sc to marker, sl st into 1 ch. Cut yarn and sew in using a tapestry needle.

For lining

Cut out 3 pieces of fabric: a rectangle 9 x 3½ inches (23 x 9 cm) and another 12 x 2 inches (30 x 5 cm) for the sides (two are needed to fit the flared shape of the pot) and a disk 2½ inches (6 cm) in diameter for the base.

Fold both rectangles in half with right sides facing and short ends matching. Stitch by machine or by hand, taking ½ inch (1 cm) seam allowance, to form a cylinder. Press the seams open. Snip into the seam allowance of the disk at short intervals, then pin it into the narrower cylinder at one end, with right sides facing. Stitch the disk to the cylinder (you may find this easier to do by hand). Now place the remaining cylinder over the first one, with right sides together and raw edges matching. Pin them together, gathering up the fullness in the wider one to fit the narrower edge. Baste, then stitch, taking ½ inch (1 cm) seam allowance. Press the seam allowances downwards, and press under ½ inch (1 cm) on the top edge. Insert the lining into the pot and stitch the folded edge just below the edging.

Yellow bowl

By working some rows through both the front and back loop of each stitch and other rows into the back loop only, you will create a ridged texture around your bowl.

Round 1 start with a slip ring, ch 1, 8 sc into ring, sl st into 1 ch, pull thread end to close ring.

Round 2 (insert marker) 2 sc into back loop only of each st to marker.

Round 3 as round 2.

Round 4 1 sc into back loop only of each st to marker.

Round 5 working into back loop only of each st, * 1 sc into next st, 2 sc into following st *, repeat from * to * to marker.

Round 6 working through both loops of each st, 1 sc into each st to marker.

Round 7 as round 6.

Round 8 1 sc into back loop only of each st to marker.

Round 9 working into back loop only of each st, * 1 sc into each of next 3 sts, 2 sc into following st *, repeat from * to * to marker.

Rounds 10 and 11 1 sc into both loops of each st to marker.

Rounds 12 and 13 1 sc into back loop only of each st to marker.

Round 14 working into back loop only of each st, *

1 sc into each of next 5 sts, 2 sc into following st *, repeat from * to * to marker.

Rounds 15 and 16 1 sc into both loops of each st to marker.

Rounds 17 and 18 1 sc into back loop only of each st to marker.

Round 19 working into both loops, 1 sc into each of next 6 sts, 2 sc into following st *, repeat from * to * to marker.

Round 20 1 sc into both loops of each st to marker. Fasten off.

Round 21 attach contrasting yarn to top edge, ch 1, 1 sc to marker, sl st into 1 ch. Fasten off.

For lining

Cut out a rectangle 14 x 3 inches (35 x 7.5 cm). Cut out a square 3½ x 3½ inches (9 x 9 cm), fold it into quarters, and trim the corners in a curve to make a disk 3½ inches (9 cm) in diameter for the base. Stitch the two short ends of the rectangle together with right sides facing. Run a line of gathering stitches around one (lower) edge of the rectangle, ½ inch (1 cm) from the raw edge, leaving the thread end free. Pull up the gathers so that this edge measures about 8½ inches (22 cm) around. Wind the thread end around a pin to secure it, and distribute the gathers evenly. Placing right sides together, pin this edge to the disk, ½ inch (1 cm) from its edge. Stitch the two pieces together by hand or machine. Place the lining in the bowl, turn under the free edge and slipstitch in place below the edging.

BUD VASE COLLARS

As the children sat drinking their favorite juice at our friends' deli on the quay in Poole, Dorset, I marveled at the miniature glass bottles with their pretty faceted bottoms. They seemed too pretty to throw into the recycling, so we brought them home and filled them with flowers. Then I crocheted some little collars to give them extra charm. As upcycling goes, it really doesn't get any easier than this. All you need is some left-over yarn, a jam jar, and a crochet hook. I like to use a mixture of colors, but you can theme a table beautifully by coordinating your yarns. I've created three slightly different patterns. They work on any size jar; simply work a length of chains long enough to stretch around the top of your jar, then join with a slip stitch to form a ring, and then follow whichever pattern you prefer. If you find yourself with two stitches left (in other words, not enough to do another petal but one stitch too many), just skip two stitches and join with a slip stitch to the base of the first petal.

YOU WILL NEED

Medium-weight cotton yarn, such as Rowan Cotton Glacé; Rowan Milk Cotton DK; Sublime Soya Cotton DK: 1 x 50 g (1¾ oz) ball of any of these is more than enough to make several collars; or you can use some left-over yarn from another project

For picot edging: fine crochet cotton, size 20: 1 x 20 g ball is more than enough for edging 3 collars

Crochet hooks: 2.25 mm or B / 1 and a smaller hook (0.75 mm–1.00 mm or 12–11 steel; see Level) for the edging

Tapestry needle

GAUGE

29 sc to 4 inches (10 cm) using main yarn and larger hook

FINISHED SIZE

The small primula collar measures 4⅜ inches (11 cm) around inner edge.

The medium peony collar measures 5½ inches (14 cm) around inner edge.

The large dahlia collar measures 8 inches (20 cm) around inner edge.

LEVEL

Starting out The basic collar is quite simple. So is the picot edging, although it does take some practice to get used to crocheting with the fine cotton. Try changing to a slightly larger or smaller hook if necessary.

INSTRUCTIONS

Primula collar (small)

Using thicker yarn, ch 34, sl st into first ch.
Round 1 ch 1, sl st into top loop only of each ch, join with a sl st to first ch.
Round 2 ch 1, work into back loop only of each st, * 1 sc, 1 dc and 1 sc in next st, sl st into following st *, repeat from * to * to end, sl st into 1 ch. Fasten off.
Picot edging using finer yarn, work into back loop only of each st. Start with a sl st at the base of one of the petals, * 2 sc into next sc, 3 sc into dc, ch 3, sl st into last sc to

form picot, 2 sc into next sc, sl st into sl st at base of petal *, repeat from * to * to end, sl st into first sl st. Fasten off.

Peony collar (medium)

Using thicker yarn, ch 48, sl st into first ch.
Round 1 ch 1, sl st into top loop only of each ch, sl st into first ch.
Round 2 ch 1, work into top loop only of each st, * skip 1 st, 1 sc, 1 dc, 1 tr, 1 dc and 1 sc into next st to form petal, skip 1 st, sl st into following st *, repeat from * to *

to end, sl st into 1 ch. Fasten off.

Picot edging using finer yarn, work into back loop only of each st. * 1 sc into sl st at base of petal, 2 sc into each of next 2 sts, 2 sc, ch 3 and 1 sc into tr, 2 sc into each of next 2 sts *, repeat from * to * to end, 1 sc into last sl st, sl st into first sc. Fasten off.

Dahlia collar (large)

Using thicker yarn, ch 60, sl st into first ch.

Round 1 ch 1, sl st into top loop only of each ch, sl st into first ch.

Round 2 ch 1, working into top loop only of each st, * skip 1 st, 1 sc, 3 dc and 1 sc into next st to form petal, skip 1 st, 1 sc into next st *, repeat from * to * to end, sl st to first ch. Fasten off.

Picot edging work as for peony collar, but working the picot (2 sc, ch 3, 1 sc) into the 2nd of the 3 dc. Fasten off.

CHILDREN'S ROOMS

If there is one room where you shouldn't hold
back on color it is a child's bedroom. Pipi is
nearly ten now, and she loves bright colors.
Unfortunately for her, she has a mother who
likes to do "white on white." At least the neutral
string-colored walls are the perfect backdrop for
white stenciled butterflies and a granny
blanket singing with every color in the
rainbow. Dante's room, too, has a neutral
backdrop, but his granny square blanket, in
vibrant red, deep blue, and crisp white, is the
perfect foil to his racing cars and dinosaurs.
Make the room fun and welcoming.

This has been a true labor of love. It's one of the first projects I embarked upon when I learned to crochet two years ago. And yes, it has taken that long to complete. Partly because I like to use leftover yarn for it, and sometimes run out of this, but principally because a granny blanket is the perfect "filler" project: a relaxing alternative when I am working on something challenging. It's like crochet "down time"—you can switch off in the evening and do a square or two while listening to the radio or watching television. Pipi has been patiently waiting two winters for this blanket; looking at it now, I know it has been worth the wait. There are yarns from sweaters my mother has knitted for me and the children and yarns from projects I have made for friends' babies. Every time we look at this blanket it will bring back memories of projects (and happy times) past.

YOU WILL NEED

About 32 oz (800 g) of DK-weight yarn in various colors (for a blanket of the size shown here). You will probably need to supplement your leftovers with additional balls; these can often be found at reduced prices in yarn stores' bins of discontinued shades

For edging and joining the squares:

Color A: Rowan Handknit Cotton DK, shade 334 Delphinium: 5 x 50 g (1¾ oz) balls

Color B: Rowan Handknit Cotton DK, shade 239 Ice Water: 1 x 50 g (1¾ oz) ball

Color C: Rowan Handknit Cotton DK, shade 833 Ochre: 1 x 50 g (1¾ oz) ball

Color D: Rowan Handknit Cotton DK, shade 747 Candy Floss: 1 x 50 g (1¾ oz) ball

Crochet hook: 2.25 mm or B / 1

Tapestry needle

GAUGE

Each square measures 4¼ inches (11 cm), including the last round, worked in the joining yarn.

FINISHED SIZE

The blanket shown measures about 32 x 45 inches (81 x 114 cm).

LEVEL

Moving on A granny square is a "must do" project for any beginner wanting to get the most out of crochet. The basic technique of working these motifs can be used to make afghans, pincushions, lavender bags, bookmarks, covers for cushions or stools—in fact, the possibilities are almost endless!

INSTRUCTIONS

For each square, decide at the outset how many colors you will use, not counting the edging yarn (A), which is introduced on round 7. You need not change color for every round, but when you do wish to change color follow the instructions on page 24.

Make 70 squares as follows:
Ch 4, sl st into first ch to form a ring.
Round 1 into ring, ch 3 (counts as first dc), 2 dc, ch 3, * 3 dc, ch 3 *, repeat from * to * twice, sl st into top of 3 ch. This first round consists of 4 groups of 3 dc each (4 sides of square), separated by 4 corners formed of 3 ch each. Fasten off first color.
Round 2 attach second color to 3-ch space at any corner (see Joining new yarn, page 24). Into corner space, ch 3 (counts as first dc), 2 dc, ch 3, 3 dc, * ch 1, 3 dc into next corner space, ch 3, 3 dc into same corner space * , repeat from * to * twice, ch 1, sl st into top of 3 ch. Fasten off second color.
Round 3 attach third color to 3-ch space at any corner. Into corner space, ch 3 (counts as first dc), 2 dc, ch 3, 3 dc, * ch 1, 3 dc into 1-ch space, ch 1 into next corner space work 3 dc, ch 3, 3 dc *, repeat * to * twice, ch 1 3 dc into 1-ch space, ch 1, sl st into top of 3 ch. Fasten off third color.
Rounds 4–7 are worked in essentially the same way: each corner consists of 2 groups of 3 dc separated by 3 ch; the sides of the square consist of groups of 3 dc worked into the 1-ch spaces of previous round and separated by 1 ch. Work round 7 in the yarn you've chosen for joining and the first round of the edging (color A).

To finish
Joining the squares
Block your squares, then lay them out on the floor or on your bed in 10 rows each of 7 squares. Once you are happy with the layout, link the squares together (flat) with safety pins. Fold two adjacent vertical rows together with

wrong sides facing. Using the same color yarn as for the last round of squares, fasten the yarn at one corner and join these two rows with single crochet. Work each stitch into the two corresponding stitches of the last rounds of the paired squares, working through the adjacent (inner) loops only, which will enable the squares to lie flat. Repeat to join the remaining vertical rows. Now join the horizontal rows in the same way. Where the corners of the squares meet, work a single crochet over the top of the one joining the vertical rows. Leave a good length of yarn at the end of each row to sew into the edging once complete.

Working the edging
For each round join the new color yarn at any point along the side of your blanket.
Round 1 using color A, ch 1, 1 sc into back loop only of each st, including ch at 1-ch spaces (not into space itself), at corners work 1 sc, ch 1 and 1 sc into 2nd of 3 ch, sl st into 1 ch. Fasten off.
Round 2 using color B, 1 sc and ch 1 (counts as 1 hdc), 1 hdc into each st along each side, at corners work 1 hdc, ch 3 and 1 hdc into 1-ch space, sl st into 1 ch. Fasten off.
Round 3 using color C, repeat round 2 along each side, at corners work 2 hdc, ch 3 and 2 hdc into 3-ch space, sl st into 1 ch. Fasten off.
Round 4 using color D, ch 1, 1 sc into each st along each side, at corners work 2 sc, ch 1 and 2 sc into 3-ch space, sl st into 1 ch. Fasten off.

You can never have too many storage pots, especially if you have children, with their attendant clutter. I have endless jam jars stuffed full of pencils, crayons, tubes of paint, and so on. With this pattern I was keen to see if giving crochet more texture would also give it the strength to hold pens. Together with the tough burlap lining it appears to be up to the job.

YOU WILL NEED

Rowan Fine Milk Cotton, shade 501 Sepia: 1 x 50 (1¾ oz) g ball

For trimming: Anchor Pearl Cotton, no. 8, shade 265: 1 x 10 g ball

Crochet hooks: 2.25 mm and 1.25 mm or B / 1 and 7 steel

Tapestry needle

Lining material, such as burlap: piece at least 8¼ x 8¼ inches (21 x 21 cm)

Thread to match lining

Sewing needle

GAUGE

39 dc and 12 rows to 4 inches (10 cm)

FINISHED SIZE

The pot measures about 3½ inches (9 cm) tall and 2½ inches (6.5 cm) in diameter.

LEVEL

Moving on This little pot is crocheted all in one piece, so you will move from crocheting a flat base to building height in the round and adding texture with the clusters of double crochet.

INSTRUCTIONS

Base

Round 1 using larger hook and Milk Cotton, make a slip ring, ch 3 (counts as 1 dc), 11 dc into ring, sl st into top of 3 ch (12 sts).

Round 2 working into back loop only of each st, ch 3 (counts as 1 dc), 1 dc into same st, 2 dc into each st, sl st into top of 3 ch (24 sts).

Round 3 as round 2 (48 sts).

Round 4 working into back loop only of each st, ch 3 (counts as 1 dc), 1 dc into same st, * 1 dc into each of next 3 sts, 2 dc into following st *, repeat from * to *, ending 1 dc into each of last 3 sts, sl st into top of 3 ch (60 sts).

Sides

Round 5 working into back loop of each st, ch 3 (counts as 1 dc), 1 dc into each of next 2 sts, 5 dc into next st, sl st behind the 5 dc into back loop only of first of the 5 dc to form bobble, * 1 dc into each of next 3 sts, 1 bobble into following st *, repeat from * to *, sl st into top of 3 ch.

Round 6 ch 1, 1 sc into top of 3 ch, 1 sc into each of next 2 dc, 1 sc over sl st at back of bobble, * 1 sc into each of next 3 dc, 1 sc over sl st at back of bobble *, repeat from * to *, sl st into 1 ch.

Round 7 ch 3, * 1 bobble into next st, 1 dc into each of following 3 sts *, repeat from * to *, ending 1 bobble into next st, 1 dc into each of last 2 sts, sl st into top of 3 ch.

Round 8 ch 1, 1 sc into top of 3 ch, * 1 sc over sl st at back of bobble, 1 sc into each of next 3 dc *, repeat from * to *, ending 1 sc over sl st at back of bobble, 1 sc into each of last 2 dc, sl st into 1 ch.

Round 9 as round 5, but working into both loops of each st. Repeat rounds 6–9 twice, then work round 6 again. Fasten off. If you would like to make your pot taller, simply add more rounds. (Of course, you will need to adjust the lining measurements.)

To make the lining

From the lining fabric cut one piece 8¼ x 4¼ inches (21 x 11 cm) and a disk about 3¼ inches (8 cm) in diameter. (Draw around an object of this size, such as a can, or around a pattern cut from paper.) Stitch the shorter ends of the rectangle together, taking ½ inch (1 cm) seam allowance, to form a cylinder. Press the seam open. Turn ½ inch (1 cm) to the wrong side along one free edge; press. Snip into the edge of the disk to a depth of about ¼ inch (5 mm), at intervals of about ¾ inch (2 cm). Pin the disk into the remaining edge of the cylinder and hand-sew it in place with small running stitches or backstitch, again taking about ½ inch (1 cm) seam allowance. Snip around the edge seam allowance of the cylinder to make it flexible.

To finish

With wrong sides together, place the lining in the pot, pushing the lower seam well down inside it. Using smaller hook and Pearl Cotton, work 1 sc into each st around top of pot, passing the hook and yarn through the lining fabric also to fix it in place. Finish with a final round of 1 sc into each st. Cut the thread and sew it into the work with a tapestry needle.

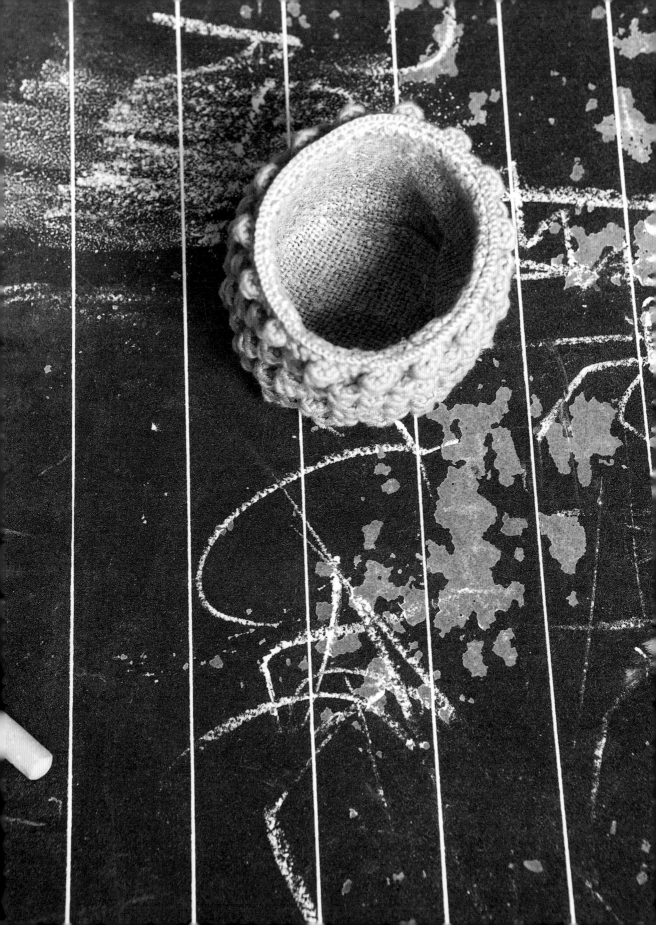

When I picked up my knitting needles again, a couple of years ago, primarily to knit baby gifts for friends, my two children found patterns for knitted bunnies, which they both requested. Even though they're growing up fast, they still adore their bunnies, and these are always the first things into the suitcase when we head off on our travels. By now, they've needed several repairs, mainly along the seams (hand-sewing is not my forte). What I love about "Olympia" is that, being crocheted in the round, she requires a minimum of sewing up. The dress itself is very simple, but the edging and little flower are a bit more challenging; accessorize within your comfort zone.

YOU WILL NEED

For the bunny:

Debbie Bliss Baby Cashmerino, shade 100 White: 1 x 50 g (1¾ oz) ball

Crochet hooks: 3.5 mm and 3.25 mm or E / 4 and D / 3

Tapestry needle

Washable polyester fiber for stuffing

Dark brown no. 8 Pearl Cotton, such as Anchor, shade 360, for eyes: small amount

Red crayon for nose and cheeks

Horsehair or nylon thread for whiskers: a few strands, about 12 inches (30 cm) long

For the dress:

Color A: Rowan Purelife Organic Cotton DK, shade 997 Light Brazilwood: 1 x 50 g (1¾ oz) ball

Color B: Rowan Siena 4-ply, shade 675 Madras: 1 x 50 g (1¾ oz) ball

Crochet hooks: 3.50 mm and 0.75 mm or E / 4 and 12 steel

Anchor 80 Crochet Cotton, shade 751: 1 x 5 g ball

Piece of pink nylon net, 36 x 8 inches (90 x 20 cm)

Pink sewing thread

Tapestry needle

Sewing needle

GAUGE

Bunny: 24 sts and 25 rows of sc to 4 inches (10 cm) on smaller hook

Dress: 23 sc to 4 inches (10 cm) on larger hook

FINISHED SIZE

Bunny measures 10 inches (25 cm) from top of head to feet.

Dress measures 4¼ inches (11 cm) long, excluding ruffle.

LEVEL

Starting out "Olympia" is worked entirely in single crochet and mainly in the round, apart from her ears, which are worked in rows, so it's good practice for both those techniques.

INSTRUCTIONS

THE BUNNY
Body
Leave a long end at end of each section for sewing up.

Round 1 using smaller hook, start with a slip ring, ch 1, 7 sc into ring, sl st into first sc. Mark last st of round with a contrasting thread and move marker up at the end of each round.

Round 2 2 sc into each st to end.

Round 3 * 1 sc into next st, 2 sc into following st *, repeat from * to * to end.

Rounds 4 and 5 * 1 sc into next st, 2 sc into following st *, repeat from * to * to last st, 1 sc into last st.

Rounds 6–12 1 sc into each sc.

Round 13 * 1 sc into each of next 5 sts, skip 1 st *, repeat from * to * to end. (Don't worry if you don't have an exact multiple of 5 stitches at the end.)

Rounds 14–19 repeat round 6.

Round 20 repeat round 13.

Rounds 21–24 repeat round 6.

Rounds 25–28 * 1 sc into each of next 4 sts, skip 1 st *, repeat from * to * to end. Fasten off. Turn right side out.

Head

Round 1 using smaller hook, start with a slip ring, ch 1, 6 sc into ring, sl st into first sc. Mark last st of round with a contrasting thread and move marker up at the end of each round.

Round 2 work into back loop only of each st, 1 sc into each st to end (this will form the little nose).

Rounds 3 and 4 2 sc into each st to end.

Round 5 * 1 sc into next st, 2 sc into following st *, repeat from * to * to end.

Rounds 6–11 1 sc into each st to end.

Round 12 * 1 sc into each of next 6 sts, skip 1 st *, repeat from * to * to end.

Round 13 repeat round 6.

Round 14 * 1 sc into each of next 4 sts, skip 1 st *, repeat from * to * to end.

Round 15 * 1 sc into each of next 3 sts, skip 1 st *, repeat from * to * to end.

Round 16 * 1 sc into each of next 2 sts, skip 1 st *, repeat from * to * to end.
Stuff the head firmly.

Rounds 17 and 18 * 1 sc in next st, skip 1 st *, repeat from * to * to end. Fasten off.

Ears
Using larger hook ch 8.

Row 1 1 sc into 2nd ch from hook, 1 sc into each ch to end, turn.

Rows 2–5 ch 1, 1 sc into each st to last st, 2 sc into last st, turn.

Rows 6–9 ch 1, 1 sc into each st to end, turn.

Row 10 ch 1, skip 1 st, 1 sc into each st to last 2 sts, skip 1 st, 1 sc into last st, turn.

Row 11 ch 1, 1 sc into each st to end, turn.

Rows 12–17 repeat rows 10 and 11 three times.

Row 18 ch 1, skip 1 st, 1 sc into each of next 2 sts, turn.

Row 19 ch 1, 1 sc into each of next 2 sts, turn.

Row 20 ch 1, skip 1 st, 1 sc into last st. Fasten off.

Arms

Round 1 using larger hook, start with a slip ring, ch 1, 7 sc into ring, sl st into first sc. Mark last st of round with a contrasting thread and move marker up at the end of each round.

Round 2 work into back loop only of each st, * 1 sc into next st, 2 sc into following st *, repeat from * to * to end.

Rounds 3–18 1 sc into each st to end.

Round 19 * 1 sc into each of next 2 sts, 2 sc into following st *, repeat from * to * to end. Fasten off.

Legs

Round 1 using larger hook, start with a slip ring, ch 1, 8 sc into ring, sl st in first sc. Mark last st of round with a contrasting thread and move marker up at end of each round.

Round 2 * 1 sc into next st, 2 sc into following st *, repeat from * to * to end.

Rounds 3–22 1 sc into each st to end.

Round 23 * 1 sc into each of next 3 sts, 2 sc into following st *, repeat from * to * to end.

Round 24 1 sc into each st to end. Fasten off. Turn right side out.

To finish

Stuff the body, arms, and legs firmly. Place the head and body together, and, using a tapestry needle, join them neatly with about 10 overcasting stitches. Close the top edge of each arm and leg, again using overcasting stitches, to produce a flat edge. Sew this edge of arms

to shoulder, where head joins body, working across the upper side and back across the lower side, with about 5 stitches in one direction and 5 in the other. Sew legs at base of body. Fold each ear in half along foundation row so that it curves inward and overcast edges. Sew to sides of head.

For Olympia's eyes, embroider a simple cross stitch, using dark brown Pearl Cotton and a tapestry needle. Color her cheeks and nose with the red crayon.

For each whisker, thread a single strand of horsehair or nylon thread through her nose. Knot the whisker on one side, then thread this end back through the nose. Trim the two ends to the desired length. For the next whisker, repeat this process, but tying the knot on the other side of the nose. Continue, alternating the position of the knots to avoid an unbalanced effect, until you have the desired number of whiskers. The knots will hold the whiskers securely in place.

THE DRESS
Bodice front and back (both alike)
Using Color A and larger hook, ch 19.

Row 1 1 hdc into 3rd ch from hook, 1 hdc into each ch to end, turn.

Row 2 ch 1, 1 sc into back loop only of each st, 1 sc into 2nd of 2 ch, turn.

Row 3 ch 1, sl st into each of first 2 sts, 1 sc into next st, 1 hdc into each of next 2 sts, sl st into each of next 8 sts, 1 hdc into each of next 2 sts, 1 sc into next st, turn. Work on last 3 sts for shoulder strap.

Row 4 ch 1, 1 hdc into each 2 hdc, turn.

Row 5 ch 1, 1 sc into each of 2 hdc, turn.

Rows 6 and 7 ch 1, 1 sc into each of 2 sc, turn.
Fasten off. Re-attach yarn to hdc at neck edge on row 3.

Rows 4–7 work as given for first shoulder strap.
Join side seams.

Skirt
Attach Color B to lower edge of bodice at center back.

Round 1 using larger hook, ch 1, 1 sc into each ch along lower edge of bodice, sl st into first sc.

Round 2 attach Color A, but do not cut off Color B (leave both colors attached throughout). ch 1, 1 sc into each st to end, sl st into first sc.
Continue working into front loop of each st on every round.

Round 3 using Color B, ch 1 * 1 sc into next st, 2 sc into following st *, repeat from * to * to end, sl st into first sc.

Round 4 using Color A, ch 1, 1 sc into each st to end, sl st into first sc.

Round 5 using Color A, ch 2, skip st at base of ch, 1 hdc into each st to end.

Round 6 using Color B, ch 1, * 1 sc into each of next 4 sts, 2 sc into following st *, repeat from * to * to end, sl st into first sc.

Round 7 using Color B, 1 sc into each st to end, sl st into first sc.

Round 8 repeat round 4.

Round 9 repeat round 5.

Round 10 using Color B, ch 1, * 1 sc into next 3 sts, 2 sc into following st *, repeat from * to * to end, sl st into first sc.

Round 11 repeat round 7.

Round 12 repeat round 4.

Round 13 repeat round 5. Fasten off.

Neck edging
Round 1 using smaller hook, attach the fine cotton at top edge of center back of bodice, ch 1, work in sc evenly around the neckline, sl st into first sc.

Round 2 * 1 sc and 1 hdc into next st, 3 dc into following st, 1 hdc and 1 sc into next st, skip 1 st, sl st in next st, skip 1 st *, repeat from * to * to end, sl st into first sc.
Fasten off.

Armhole edging
Round 1 using smaller hook, attach fine cotton at underarm seam, ch 1, work in sc evenly around armhole, sl st into first sc.

Round 2 ch 1, 1 sc into each st, sl st into first sc.
Fasten off.

Corsage
Using smaller hook and fine cotton, start with a slip ring, ch 3, 11 dc into slip ring, sl st into top of 3 ch, pull ring tight.
Petals * 1 sc, 3 dc, 1 sc into next st, sl st into following st *, repeat from * to * to end, sl st into first sc. Fasten off.

Net petticoat
Cut the piece of net into 4 long strips. Lay the strips one on top of the other and baste them together along one straight long edge. Using pink sewing thread and a tapestry needle and small overcasting stitches, hand-sew this edge to the wrong side of the dress just above the top of round 11 (final round of Color B), gathering it as you sew.

OUT OF DOORS

Our life in Dorset is spent very much in the great outdoors. Come rain or shine, we will be out foraging, whether it's for autumn mushrooms or summer samphire. The children love paddling at the harbor's edge; and we all like nothing better than to eat alfresco—in the garden, with The Sicilian grilling fish and vegetables on the barbecue, or spread out on a blanket at the beach, enjoying a delicious picnic. Make your outdoor living just as stylish as your home with little touches of crochet magic.

Maybe it's the Italian in me, but from a very young age I have hankered after a Fiat Cinquecento. I remember passing a garage in Battersea, London, on the top deck of the No. 137 bus, and gazing down at the little battered rust buckets being lovingly restored. Unfortunately, living in the country, with next to no public transportation, obliges me to do far too much driving, and one of those old 500s simply wouldn't have been up to it. Then, to my delight, Fiat bought out a new version. Mine is a little green one, dubbed Agnes. The only downside to my cheeky little car is the cream dashboard and steering wheel, which in spite of my best efforts always end up a dirty shade of gray. Hence the crocheted leather cover. I think it adds just another layer of sophistication and practicality to my super-gorgeous, low-emission, fabulously easy-to-park Agnes.

YOU WILL NEED

Leather cord, 1/16 inch (1 mm) diameter: about 55 yards (50 m)

Leather cord, 1/8 inch (2 mm) diameter: about 11 yards (10 m)

Crochet hook: 3.5 mm or E / 4

Large tapestry needle

GAUGE

Gauge is not critical for this project.

FINISHED SIZE

The cover shown fits a steering wheel of about 45 inches (114 cm) circumference.

LEVEL

Starting out Super-simple. You may find the leather a bit stiff at the beginning, but you will soon get used to it.

INSTRUCTIONS

Starting with a slip knot, ch 18.

Foundation row 1 dc into 8th ch from hook, * ch 5, skip 4 ch, 1 dc into next ch *, repeat from * to * once, turn.

Row 1 ch 5, 1 dc into first ch space, * ch 5, 1 dc into next ch space *, repeat from * to * once, turn.

Repeat row 1 until the strip of leather lattice is long enough to go around your steering wheel. In the case of my 500, 64 repeats were required.

To finish

Using the thicker leather cord in a tapestry needle, lace your cover onto your steering wheel.

A project that combines linen, crochet and Liberty fabric is always going to be one of my favorites. "Betsy" is a classic Liberty Tana Lawn, but whatever fabric you select to line your summer bag, coordinate it with your cotton yarn for maximum effect.

YOU WILL NEED

For pink flower: Anchor Artiste Mercer Crochet thread no. 20, shade 893: 1 x 20 g ball

For large green flower: Anchor Artiste Mercer thread no. 20, shade 206: 1 x 20 g ball

For smaller green flower: Anchor Pearl Cotton no. 8, shade 265: 1 x 10 g ball

For turquoise flower: Anchor Pearl Cotton no. 8, shade 186: 1 x 10 g ball

Crochet hook: 1.00 mm or 11 steel

Tapestry needle

Linen fabric at least 36 inches (92 cm) wide: ½ yard (40 cm)

Lining fabric at least 36 inches (92 cm) wide, such as Tana Lawn "Betsy": ½ yard (40 cm)

Medium-weight polyester batting at least 36 inches (92 cm) wide: ½ yard (40 cm)

Spray adhesive

Sewing needle or chenille needle

Sewing thread to match motifs

Sewing machine

Pair of D-shaped natural bamboo handles, 8 inches (20 cm) wide

GAUGE

Gauge is not critical on this project.

FINISHED SIZE

The handbag measures about 17 x 12 inches (43 x 30 cm).

LEVEL

Moving on Creating motifs is a wonderful way to experiment with new stitches. If at first you don't succeed, try again; you'll be amazed at how many uses you can find for your motifs—lavender bags, jute shopping bags, and pillowcases are just some of the possibilities.

INSTRUCTIONS

Pink flower

Ch 6, sl st into first ch to close.

Round 1 ch 5 (counts as 1 dc and 2 ch), * 1 dc into center of ring, ch 2 *, repeat from * to * 7 times, sl st into 3rd of 5 ch (9 ch spaces).

Round 2 into each ch space, work 1 sc, 3 dc and 1 sc, sl st into first sc (9 petals).

Round 3 working into the back of the petals, * sl st into the vertical strand at the back of first sc of petal of last round, ch 3 *, repeat from * to * into each petal, sl st into same place as first sl st.

Round 4 1 sc, 5 dc and 1 sc into each ch space, sl st into first sc.

Round 5 working into petals of round 4, work as round 3, but working ch 5 instead of ch 3.

Round 6 work as round 4, but working 7 dc instead of 5 dc. Fasten off.

Large green flower

Round 1 start with a slip ring, ch 4 (counts as 1 tr), 19 tr into ring, sl st into top of 4 ch (20 sts).

Round 2 ch 5 (counts as 1 dtr), working into back loop only of each st, 1 dtr into same st, 2 dtr into each tr of previous round, sl st into top of 5 ch.

Round 3 ch 3, working into back loop only of each st, 1 dc into each of next 3 sts, ch 4, * 1 dc into each of next 4 sts, ch 4 *, repeat from * to *, sl st into top of 3 ch.

Round 4 sl st into back loop only of next 3 dc and into ch space, ch 3, 2 dc, ch 4 and 3 dc into same ch space, * ch 4, 3 dc, ch 4, 3 dc into next ch space *, repeat from * to *, ending ch 4, sl st into top of 3 ch.

Round 5 sl st into back loop only of next 2 dc and into ch space, ch 3, 2 dc, ch 4 and 3 dc into same ch space, * ch 6, 3 dc, ch 4, 3 dc into next ch space *, repeat from * to *, ending ch 6, sl st into top of 3 ch.

Round 6 sl st into back loop only of next 2 dc and into ch space, ch 3, 2 dc, ch 3 and 3 dc into same ch space, * ch 4, 1 sc incorporating 6 ch and 4 ch of 2 previous rounds, ch 4, 3 dc, ch 3 and 3 dc into next ch space *, repeat

from * to *, ending ch 4, 1 sc incorporating 6 ch and 4 ch of 2 previous rounds, ch 4, sl st into top of 3 ch. Fasten off.

Smaller green flower

Round 1 start with a slip ring, ch 4 (counts as 1 tr), 17 tr into ring, pull tight and close with a sl st into 4 ch (18 sts).

Round 2 ch 3, 1 dc into same place as sl st, 2 dc into back loop only of each tr, sl st into top of 3 ch.

Round 3 * ch 3, skip 1 st, 1 sc into back loop only of next st *, repeat from * to *, ending ch 3, skip last st, sl st into st at base of 3 ch.

Round 4 sl st into each of first 2 ch, * ch 5, sl st into second of 3 ch (middle of arch) *, repeat from * to *, ending ch 5, sl st into first ch.

Round 5 sl st into next ch, 1 sc into next ch, * ch 5, 1 sc into 3rd ch of arch *, repeat from * to *, ending ch 5, sl st into first sc.

Round 6 5 sc into each ch space, sl st into first sc.

Round 7 ch 3, 1 dc into back loop only of each st, sl st into top of 3 ch.

Round 8 * working into back loop only of each st, 1 sc into next st, 1 dc into next st, 1 tr into next st, ch 2, 1 tr into next st, 1 dc into next st, 1 sc into next st, sl st into next st *, repeat from * to * to end. Fasten off.

Turquoise flower

Round 1 start with a slip ring, ch 4 (counts as 1 tr), 17 tr into ring, pull tight and close with sl st into top of 4 ch (18 sts).

Round 2 ch 4, 1 tr into same place as sl st, 2 tr into each tr, sl st into top of 4 ch.

Round 3 ch 1, 1 sc into back loop only of each tr, sl st into 1 ch.

Round 4 ch 5 (counts as 1 dc, 2 ch), * skip next st, 1 dc into next st, ch 2, 1 dc into next st, ch 2 *, repeat from * to *, ending sl st into 3rd of 5 ch (24 ch spaces).

Round 5 * 1 sc, 1 hdc, 1 dc, 1 tr, 1 dc, 1 hdc and 1 sc

all into next dc, sl st into next dc *, repeat from * to *, ending sl st into same place as sl st at end of last round. Fasten off.

To finish

Cut 2 pieces of main bag fabric, each 18 inches (46 cm) wide and 15 inches (38 cm) high. Cut 2 pieces of lining fabric the same size. Cut 2 pieces of batting, each 18 inches (46 cm) wide and 13 inches (33 cm) high. Using a flat, round object as a template (I used a plate with an 18-inch [46-cm] diameter) and a pencil, mark a curve on the lower two corners of each piece of fabric on the wrong side. Trim along these lines, then, using one fabric piece as a pattern, trim the batting pieces to match. Using spray adhesive, stick one batting piece to the wrong side of each main bag section. (Note that the batting stops 2 inches [5 cm] from the top edge.)

Position the motifs on the right side of one bag section as shown (or to suit your own taste). Pin them in place and use a tapestry or sewing needle to take the beginning thread to the wrong side; fasten it to the batting with a few stitches. Use matching sewing thread and a sharp-pointed sewing or chenille needle to stitch the edges of each motif invisibly to the bag fabric (it is all right to include some of the batting in these stitches). Using the crochet cotton and a sharp-pointed needle, work running-stitch stems from the lower edge up to each flower (work stem in a different color from flower), stitching through both fabric and batting.

Pin the two main bag sections together with right sides facing, and stitch them together along their lower and side edges, taking ½ inch (1 cm) seam allowance and beginning and ending 6 inches (15 cm) down from the straight top edge. Clip the curved edges at short intervals. Pin the two lining sections together, right sides facing, and stitch them together along their side edges (taking ½ inch

[1 cm] seam allowance), again leaving 6 inches (15 cm) free below the top edges but also leaving a gap of about 8 inches (20 cm) in the center of the bottom edge. Clip the curved edges.

Turn the main bag piece right side out, leaving the lining wrong side out. Slip the bag into the lining and push it down until their top and upper side edges are aligned. Pin and machine-stitch these edges together (baste, too, if you like), taking ½ inch (1 cm) seam allowances. Trim the seam allowances and press them flat (this embeds the stitches for a neater finish).

Now pull the bag through the gap in the lining. At this point, both bag and lining will be right side out. Turn in the raw edges of the lining gap and press them in place. Topstitch them together, close to the fold. Push the lining down into the bag. Press the top and upper side seams flat for a nice crisp finish.

Turn 2 inches (5 cm) of each top edge over a handle, lining side out as shown, and pin and baste it in place. You will need to bunch it up slightly to fit the straight part of the handle. Then, using a harmonizing thread in a sewing or chenille needle, backstitch through all layers. It is impossible to do this by machine, because of the bulk. Work backward and forward several times to make the hem secure. Be patient and sew carefully.

My handbag is a seemingly bottomless chasm—
I am forever rummaging amid pens, notepads,
crochet hooks, and more; so I finally realized
that my smartphone needed to be kept safe
from scratches. This little cover, decorated
with crocheted motifs, makes it easier to spot,
too. Such a small project lends itself to left-over
fabrics; I've used some of the deep blue boiled
wool left from Pipi's winter coat and lined it
with my favorite "Betsy" Liberty Tana Lawn.
The only challenge for me was the Dorset
button I used for the fastening. I'd attended
two workshops on these little wheel-shaped
buttons (traditionally made in the county of
Dorset), but without finishing one button.
But I do recommend trying one; they are so
satisfying and give the cover an elegant finish
(see page 141 for a website offering instructions
on making them). If you prefer, you can, of
course, use a purchased new or vintage button.

YOU WILL NEED

For blue motif: Anchor Aida 6-ply Crochet Thread no.
10, shade 0850: 1 x 50 g (1¾ oz) ball

For pink motifs: Anchor Artiste Mercer Crochet thread
no. 20, shade 0968: 1 x 20 g ball

For pale green motif: Anchor Artiste Mercer thread
no. 20, shade 1042: 1 x 20 g ball

(Note: a single ball of any of these would be enough for
all three motifs.)

Crochet hooks: 1.0 mm and 0.75 mm or 11 and 12 steel

Piece of fabric for outer cover, to fit around front and
back of smartphone, plus 1¼ inches (3 cm), and to fit
from top to bottom, plus 1¼ inches (3 cm)

Piece of lining fabric, same size as outer cover

Purchased button (or plastic ring for making a Dorset
button)

Tapestry needle

Chenille needle or other large-eyed, sharp-pointed
needle

Sewing needle

Sewing thread to match outer cover and motifs

Sewing machine (optional)

GAUGE

Gauge is not critical for this project.

FINISHED SIZE

To fit smartphone comfortably; the cover shown here
measures 5 x 3¼ inches (12.5 x 8 cm).

LEVEL

Moving on Each motif is quite simple once you have
mastered slip rings and working in the round.

INSTRUCTIONS

Blue motif
Round 1 start with a slip ring, 1 sc, ch 3 (counts as 1 tr)
into ring, 15 tr into ring, sl st into top of 3 ch. Pull tail to
close ring (16 sts).

Round 2 ch 4 (counts as 1 tr) and 1 tr into same st, *
ch 1, 2 tr into next st *, repeat from * to *, ch 1, sl st into
top of 4 ch.

Round 3 sl st across top of 2 tr, into next ch space work

1 sc, ch 3 (counts as 1 tr), and 1 tr, ch 3, * 2 tr into next ch space, ch 3 *, repeat from * to *, sl st into top of 3 ch.
Round 4 ch 1, 1 sc into back loop only of each st of previous round, sl st into 1 ch.
Round 5 ch 1, *1 sc into next st, 1 dc into following st, 2 tr into next st, 1 dc into following st, 1 sc into next st, ch 1, skip 1 st, 1 sc into next st, ch 1, skip 1 st *, repeat from * to * to beginning, sl st into 1 ch to finish. Fasten off.

Pink motif (on front of cover)

Round 1 start with a slip ring, 1 sc, ch 2 (counts as 1 dc) into slip ring, 13 dc into ring, sl st into top of 2 ch (14 sts). Pull tail to close ring.
Round 2 ch 4 (counts as 1 dc, 1 ch), * 1 dc and ch 1 into back loop of next dc *, repeat from * to *, sl st into 3rd of 4 ch.
Round 3 1 sc into next ch space, * ch 3, 1 sc into next ch space *, repeat from * to *, ch 3, sl st into first sc.
Round 4 ch 1, into each ch space work 1 sc, 3 dc and 1 sc to form petals, sl st into 1 ch. Fasten off.

Pink motif (on back of cover)

Round 1 start with a slip ring, 1 sc, ch 2 (counts as 1 dc) into slip ring, 15 dc into ring, sl st into top of 2 ch (16 sts). Pull tail to close ring.
Round 2 ch 4 (counts as 1 tr) and 1 tr into same st, * 2 tr into next st *, repeat from * to *, sl st into top of 4 ch.
Round 3 * ch 2, 1 sc in between this tr and next tr *, repeat from * to *, sl st into 1 ch to finish. Fasten off.

Pale green motif

Round 1 start with a slip ring, 1 sc, ch 3 (counts as 1 tr) into ring, 15 tr into ring, sl st into top of 3 ch (16 sts). Pull tail to close ring.
Round 2 ch 4 (counts as 1 tr), 1 tr into same st, 2 tr into each tr, sl st into top of 4 ch.
Round 3 ch 1, * working into back loop only, 1 sc into next tr, 2 tr into following tr *, repeat from * to * to end, sl st into 1 ch.
Round 4 ch 6 (counts as 1 dc, 3 ch), skip next st, * 1 dc

in back loop of next st, ch 3, skip next st *, repeat from * to *, sl st into 3rd of 6 ch.
Round 5 ch 1, then into each ch space work 1 sc, 3 dc and 1 sc to form petals, sl st into 1 ch. Fasten off.

To finish

Begin by sewing your motifs to the outer fabric, first wrapping it around the phone to decide on the best positions. Use a chenille or other sharp-pointed needle to bring the starting yarn through to the wrong side, and fasten it in place securely. Use a sewing needle and matching thread to anchor the motifs around the edges; this will prevent them from getting wrinkled.

Fold the fabric in half, right sides facing, matching the shorter edges. Stitch along these edges, taking ½ inch (1 cm) seam allowance. (Use a machine or small backstitches.) Stitch along one remaining edge to form the bottom seam. Clip diagonally across the corner where the seams meet to reduce bulk. Press the seams open and turn the cover right side out. Turn under and press ½ inch (1 cm) on the remaining (top) edge.

Sew the button in the center of one side of the cover, about 5/8 inch (1.5 cm) down from the pressed edge. Using crochet cotton, work a length of chain long enough to go from just below the seam allowance on the opposite side, around the button, and back (here, about 3¼ inches [8 cm]). Fasten off. Thread the two ends into a chenille needle, take them through to the wrong side of the back of the cover, and fasten securely. I covered the "exit" point of the loop on the back with a pink crochet motif.

Make the lining in the same way as the outer cover, but leave it wrong side out. Slip it into the outer cover with the seam in the folded edge (to avoid the bulk of two superimposed seams). Push it well down into the corners. If necessary, fold under a bit more of the top edge, then slipstitch the lining and outer cover together with tiny stitches.

A curly scarf was one of the first crochet projects I tried. They look so complicated, but actually the simple action of increasing the number of stitches as you work along a straight row (the scarf is worked sideways) will cause your work to curl naturally. I like to use a lightweight yarn, such as mohair, lace weight, or, as here, a kid mohair-silk blend, to give the scarf an ethereal quality. Pipi loves the way it tickles her chin, and despite seeming like a cobweb, it keeps her toasty warm.

YOU WILL NEED

Rowan Kidsilk Haze, shade 589 Majestic: 1 x 25 g (1 oz) ball

Crochet hook: 4 mm or G / 6

Crystal beads, such as Swarovski 3 mm Grey Opal: about 230

Tapestry needle

GAUGE

20 sc to 4 inches (10 cm)

FINISHED SIZE

Scarf measures about 43 inches (1.1 m) long.

LEVEL

Moving on It can be a challenge working with a fluffy yarn; the key is to use a relatively large hook and keep your tension loose. Make sure that the beads you select have a hole large enough for the yarn to go through.

INSTRUCTIONS

Begin by threading all of the beads onto your yarn (see page 26).

Ch 150.

Foundation row 1 sc into 2nd ch from hook, 1 sc into each ch to end, turn.

Row 1 working into front loop only of each st, ch 3, skip first st, 1 hdc and ch 1 into each st to last st, 1 hdc into last st, turn.

Row 2 working into back loop only of each st, 3 sc into first st, * 1 sc into each of next 3 sts, 3 sc into next st *, repeat from * to * to end, turn.

Row 3 working into front loop only of each st, 1 sc into first st, * 1 sc into next st, ch 1, slide a bead up to last st, work ch 1 on far side of bead to hold bead in place, sl st into first of last 2 ch, 1 sc into same place as last sc, 1 sc into each of next 5 sc *, repeat from * to * to end, omitting 4 sc at end of last repeat. Fasten off.

Row 4 turn work upside down and join yarn to first st.

Working into free loops of foundation row, ch 3, 1 dc into first st, 2 dc into each st to end, turn.

Row 5 working into back loop only of each st, ch 4, 1 tr into first st, 2 tr into each st to end, turn.

Row 6 working into front loop only of each st, * 1 sc into st, ch 1, slide a bead up to last st, ch 2, 1 sc into same st as last sc, 1 sc into each of next 3 sts *, repeat from * to * to end. Fasten off.

SNOWFLAKE BERET

I like to wrap up my children in the winter, and although Dante is happy to sport any hat we give him, Pipi definitely needs a bit more encouragement. This chic beret, in the softest kid mohair-silk blend, is perfect for a brisk walk, and it is so light, she might not even notice she is wearing it.

GAUGE

17 dc to 4 inches (10 cm)

FINISHED SIZE

Beret measures approximately 10½ inches (27 cm) in diameter (flat).

YOU WILL NEED

Rowan Kidsilk Haze, shade 589 Majestic: 1 x 25 g (1 oz) ball

Crochet hooks: 4.00 mm, 3.5 mm and 2.25 mm or G / 6, E / 4, and B / 1

Crystal beads, such as Swarovski, 3 mm Grey Opal: 45

Hat elastic to fit around head (optional)

Tapestry needle

LEVEL

Confident Shaping a beret and working with this fluffy (but beautiful) yarn present a few challenges. I have specified the number of stitches you should have at the end of certain rounds, but counting stitches in a fluffy yarn can be tricky. Don't worry if you are over or under by a stitch or two.

INSTRUCTIONS

Begin by threading all of the beads onto your yarn (see page 26).

Round 1 using the smallest hook, make a slip ring. ch 1, 10 sc into ring, close ring with a sl st into 1 ch.

Round 2 ch 1, 3 sc into each of 10 sc, sl st into 1 ch (30 sts).

Round 3 ch 1, * 3 sc into next sc, 2 sc into each of next 2 sc *, repeat from * to * to end, sl st into 1 ch (70 sts). Work into back loop only of each st throughout.

Round 4 change to medium-size hook, ch 3 (counts as first dc), 1 dc into first sc, * 1 dc into each of next 5 sc, 3 dc tog over next 3 sc, pulling 1 bead through with center dc, 1 dc into each of next 5 sc, (2 dc, ch 2, 2 dc) into next 1 sc *, repeat from * to *, ending with 2 dc, ch 2, into same st as first dc of round, sl st into top of 3 ch (15 sts on each side between corner 2-ch spaces).

Round 5 change to largest hook, sl st back into 2-ch space, ch 3, 1 dc into same space, * 1 dc into each st to 1 st before 3 dc tog of last round, 3 dc tog over next 3 sts, pulling 1 bead through with center dc, 1 dc into each st to next 2-ch space, (2 dc, ch 2, 2 dc) into 2-ch space *, repeat from * to *, ending 2 dc, ch 2 into same space as first dc of round, sl st in top of 3 ch.

Rounds 6–12 as round 5 (31 sts on each side between corner 2-ch spaces).

Round 13 ch 1, * 1 sc into first st, 1 hdc into each of following 5 sts, 1 dc into each of next 5 sts, 1 tr into each of following 9 sts, 1 dc into each of next 5 sts, 1 hdc into each of following 5 sts, 1 sc into next st, 2 sc into 2-ch space *, repeat from * to * to end, sl st into 1 ch (165 sts). (This round evens out the work to provide a smooth circle on which to work the decrease rounds.)

Round 14 1 sc into each st of previous round.

Rounds 15–17 1 dc into each st of previous round.

Round 18 ch 1, 1 sc into next dc, * skip 1 st, 1 sc into next st *, repeat from * to * to end, sl st in 1 ch (83 sts).

Round 19 change to smallest hook, ch 1 *, 1 sc into each of next 3 sts, skip 1 st *, repeat from * to * to last 3 sts, 1 sc into each of 3 sc, sl st in 1 ch (63 sts). Fasten off. This will bring the beret in to fit around head. (If it is too loose, sew in a length of hat elastic.)

LACY SCARF

What comes first, the pattern or the yarn? It's a bit of a chicken- and egg- question for me, and it just depends on the project. In the case of this scarf, it was definitely the yarn. I stumbled across it on the Etsy Website. The range of colors and subtlety of shades just blew me away. When the little parcel from Nuremberg, Germany, landed softly on my doormat I could hardly contain my excitement (The Sicilian thinks I'm developing an addiction to yarn). I knew as soon as I unwrapped it that I wanted it close to my skin, so I made the perfect scarf for trapping the cold winter air and warming it up beautifully.

YOU WILL NEED

DyeForYarn Tussah Silk Lace, shade Ageing Olive: 1 x 100 g (3½ oz) skein

Crochet hook: 4 mm or G / 6

Tapestry needle

GAUGE

1 pattern repeat (across) measures 1½ inches (4 cm).

3 pattern repeats (across) measures 3¼ inches (8 cm).

FINISHED SIZE

Scarf measures about 46 inches (117 cm) long and 14 inches (36 cm) wide.

LEVEL

Starting out I've given this a "beginner" rating because once you've cracked the pattern—the first 5 rows—you just repeat these, enjoying the sensation of working with such beautiful yarn. If this doesn't get you hooked on crochet, nothing will. Unlike the mohair-type yarns, this glides off your hook and is as easy to undo as it is to work.

INSTRUCTIONS

Ch 100.

Foundation row skip 5 ch, * 2 dc, ch 1, 2 dc into next ch, skip 3 ch, 2 dc, ch 1, 2 dc into next ch, ch 4, skip 6 ch *, repeat from * to *, ending 2 dc, ch 1, 2 dc into next ch, skip 3 ch, 2 dc, ch 1, 2 dc into next ch, skip next ch, 1 dc into last ch, turn.

Row 1 ch 3, * work 2 dc, ch 1, 2 dc into each of next two 1-ch spaces, ch 3, insert hook under 6-ch space of foundation ch and work 1 sc, enclosing 6-ch space and 4-ch space on foundation row, ch 3 *, repeat from * to *, ending 2 dc, ch 1, 2 dc into each of last two 1-ch spaces, 1 dc into space before turning ch, turn.

Row 2 ch 3, * work 2 dc, ch 1, 2 dc into each of next two 1-ch spaces, ch 4 *, repeat from * to *, ending 2 dc, ch 1, 2 dc into each of last two 1-ch spaces, 1 dc into space before 3 ch, turn.

Row 3 repeat row 2.

Row 4 ch 3, * 2 dc, ch 1, 2 dc into each of next two 1-ch spaces, ch 3, insert hook under 4-ch space 2 rows below and work 1 sc enclosing both 4-ch spaces, ch 3 *, repeat from * to *, ending 2 dc, ch 1, 2 dc into each of last two 1-ch spaces, 1 dc into space before 3 ch, turn.

Repeat rows 2–4 a total of 43 times. (I ran out of yarn before I could do a row 4 on the 43rd repeat, so just finished with row 3, but it doesn't detract from the pattern; just remember to sc the chain length from row 2 when working on row 3.) Fasten off.

Perfect for chilly winter days and three-quarter-length sleeves. I feel the cold, maybe because of my splash of Mediterranean blood, and am always on the lookout for comforting gloves and scarves. It is often handy to have your fingers "out," so to speak, especially if you want to crochet on the move, so wrist warmers are the perfect solution. You could do these in the same color as the lacy scarf (see page 134) for a matching set, but you will need two skeins of the same color.

YOU WILL NEED

DyeForYarn Tussah Silk Lace, shade Fading Rose: 1 x 100 g (3½ oz) skein (enough for two pairs)

Crochet hook: 2.25 mm or B / 1

Tapestry needle

GAUGE

29 hdc and 23 rows to 4 inches (10 cm)

FINISHED SIZE

About 9 inches (23 cm) long and 7½ inches (19 cm) in circumference

LEVEL

Starting out These wrist warmers are worked in the round, and apart from sewing in the ends, they require no finishing. They're also identical, so you follow the same instructions to make both.

INSTRUCTIONS

When working in rounds I normally—as here—prefer not to chain up (see page 20) for each round; but simply continuing in an unbroken spiral (using the contrasting marker to keep track of beginning/end of rounds) will give you a smoother stitch flow. However, this does mean that you need to finish the body of work with a slip stitch to bring the height in line with the last row. I will indicate each time you need to do a slip stitch.

Ch 56, sl st into first ch to form a circle, taking care not to twist ch.

Round 1 ch 2, 1 hdc into each ch, sl st into top of 2 ch. Mark last hdc of round and move marker up on every round.

Rounds 2–30 1 hdc into each st.

Divide for thumb hole

Sl st into next hdc, turn and work backward and forward in rows.

Row 1 ch 2, skip st at base of ch, 1 hdc into each st to end, turn.

Rows 2–12 as row 1, but do not turn at end of row 12. Continue in rounds.

Round 31 1 hdc into each st, mark last st of round and move marker up on every round.

Rounds 32–36 as round 31.

Round 37 start ruffle with sl st into next st, ch 3 (counts as 1 hdc, ch 1), 1 hdc into same st, skip 2 sts, 1 hdc, ch 1 and 1 hdc in next st, ch 3 skip 3 sts, * 1 hdc, ch 1 and 1 hdc in next st, skip 2 sts, 1 hdc, ch 1 and 1 hdc in next st, ch 3, skip 3 sts *, repeat from * to * 6 times, sl st into 2nd of 3 ch.

Round 38 sl st into 1-ch sp before first hdc, ch 3 (counts as 1 hdc, ch 1), 1 hdc into same space, 1 hdc, ch 1 and 1 hdc, into next 1-ch space, ch 3, * 1 hdc, ch 1 and 1 hdc into each of next two 1-ch spaces, ch 3 *, repeat from * to * 6 times, sl st into 2nd of 3 ch.

Round 39 sl st into 1-ch sp before first hdc, ch 2, 1 hdc, ch 1 and 2 hdc into same space, 2 hdc, ch 1 and 2 hdc into next 1-ch space, ch 2, work 1 sc around both 3-ch spaces below, ch 2, * 2 hdc, ch 1 and 2 hdc into each of next two 1-ch spaces, ch 2, work 1 sc around both 3-ch spaces below, 2 ch *, repeat from * to * 6 times, sl st into 2nd of 2 ch. Fasten off.

I always feel that men are a bit hard done by when it comes to crochet patterns—there aren't many, and most aren't very exciting. The Sicilian has always been quite conscious of his attire, so in designing a broomstick lace scarf for him, I needed one that would gratify his taste for subtle colors and high-quality yarn. And what could be more beautiful than my friend Jenny Taylor's hand-spun merino-silk yarn? Jenny is one of the girls in our (Corfe Castle) Wool Workshop (of knitters, crocheters, spinners, etc., in wool), and I knew she had a stash of her own yarn at home. When she presented me with one ball of this yarn, I tentatively asked if she had any more. To my delight, she had 11 ounces (270 g) of it, which, happily, she was willing to part with. If you can find this sort of hand-spun yarn, go for it. But you can make a lovely scarf using a machine-spun yarn such as the Rowan yarn I've suggested here.

YOU WILL NEED

Rowan Purelife British Sheep Breeds DK Undyed: in a color of your choice: 3 x 50 g (1¾ oz) balls for narrow scarf; 5 x 50 g (1¾ oz) balls for wide scarf

Knitting needle: 20 mm or size 35

Crochet hook: 3.5 mm or E / 4

Tapestry needle

GAUGE

6 groups of 5 loops to 4 inches (10 cm)

FINISHED SIZE

The scarves measure 59 inches (150 cm) long; narrow scarf 4¾ inches (12 cm) wide, wide scarf 8 inches (20 cm) wide.

LEVEL

Starting out Broomstick lace is a simple technique (see page 27), which consists of working stitches onto and off a large knitting needle or similar object, using a smaller crochet hook. Just choose a good bulky yarn and set to work on a long winter's evening—you'll be amazed how quickly you progress.

INSTRUCTIONS

Using the crochet hook, ch 35 for narrow scarf, ch 60 for wide scarf.

Row 1 place the loop from hook on the knitting needle, * insert hook into next ch, yarn over hook, draw loop through and slip it on the knitting needle *, repeat from * to * to end (35 loops for narrow scarf, 60 loops for wide scarf).

Row 2 * using the crochet hook, work 1 sc through the center of the first 5 loops, then work another 4 sc into the same place *, repeat from * to * to end. I find it easier to keep the loops on the knitting needle until you have worked the first sc to secure your 5 loops, then slip the group off the needle and complete the next 4 sc (7 groups for narrow scarf, 12 groups for wide scarf).

Row 3 place the loop from hook on the knitting needle, skip first sc, * insert hook into next sc, yarn over hook, draw loop through and slip it on the knitting needle *, repeat from * to * to end (35 loops for narrow scarf, 60 loops for wide scarf).

Repeat rows 2 and 3 until scarf measures 60 inches (150 cm), ending with row 2. Fasten off.

USEFUL INFORMATION

Yarns

The yarns and threads used for projects in this book are listed below. If you cannot find the specified yarn, you can substitute a similar yarn; check the length to make sure you will have enough. Also check the gauge (see page 23) obtained with the new yarn.

- Anchor Aida Crochet Cotton no. 10 (50 g, 265 m/289 yd)
- Anchor Artiste Linen no. 10 (50 g, 265 m/289 yd)
- Anchor Artiste Mercer Crochet no. 20 (20 g, 387 m/422 yd)
- Anchor Artiste Mercer Crochet no. 80 (5 g, 100 m/110 yd)
- Anchor Pearl Cotton no. 8 (10 g, 82 m/89 yd)
- Debbie Bliss Baby Cashmerino (50 g, 125 m/137 yd)
- Debbie Bliss Bella (50 g, 95 m/104 yd)
- Debbie Bliss Eco Aran Fair Trade Collection (50 g, 75 m/82 yd)
- Debbie Bliss Ecobaby Fair Trade Collection (50 g 125 m/137 yd)
- DMC Natura Just Cotton (50 g, 155 m/169 yd)
- DyeForYarn Tussah Silk Lace (100 g, 695 m/758 yd)
- Puppets Lyric 8/8 Crochet & Knitting Cotton (50 g, 70 m/76 yd)
- Rowan Pure Cashmere DK (25 g, 112 m/122 yd)
- Rowan Cotton Glace (50 g, 115 m/125 yd)
- Rowan Fine Milk Cotton (50 g, 150 m/164 yd)
- Rowan Handknit Cotton DK (50 g, 85 m/93 yd)
- Rowan Kidsilk Haze (25 g, 210 m/229 yd)
- Rowan Milk Cotton DK (50 g, 113 m/123 yd)
- Rowan Purelife British Sheep Breeds DK Undyed (50g, 120 m/131 yd)
- Rowan Purelife Organic Cotton DK (50 g, 120 m/131 yd)
- Rowan Siena 4 ply (50 g, 140 m/153 yd)
- Sirdar Snuggly Baby Bamboo DK (50 g, 95 m/104 yd)
- Sublime Soya Cotton DK (50 g, 110 m/120 yd)
- Stylecraft Craft Cotton (100g, 166 m/182 yd))
- Twilleys Freedom Sincere Organic Cotton DK (50 g, 115 m/125 yd)

The initials DK stand for "double knitting." This is a standard weight of British yarn, slightly thinner than a worsted weight and slightly thicker than a sport weight yarn. DK yarns by various British manufacturers are now becoming more widely available in the United States, and you should be able to buy them from a good yarn store or an online supplier.

Hook conversion chart

Metrically sized hooks (which are now available in the United States) were used for the projects in this book, and that is why those sizes are given first with the projects, with American sizes given as alternatives. You may find this table useful for converting metric sizes given in other patterns.

METRIC	U.S. SIZES
0.6 mm	14 steel
0.75 mm	12 steel
1 mm	11 steel
1.25 mm	7 steel
1.5 mm	6 steel
1.75 mm	5 steel
2 mm	
2.25 mm	B / 1
2.5 mm	
2.75 mm	C / 2
3 mm	
3.25 mm	D / 3
3.5 mm	E / 4
3.75 mm	F / 5
4 mm	G / 6
4.5 mm	7
5 mm	H / 8
5.5 mm	I / 9
6 mm	J / 10
6.5 mm	K / 10½
7 mm	
8 mm	L / 11
9 mm	M / 13
10 mm	N / 15
12 mm	P
15 mm	Q (16 mm)
20 mm	S (19 mm)

RESOURCES

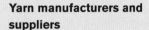

Yarn manufacturers and suppliers

The following are sources of the four most-used yarns and threads in this book. For other yarns, please search the Internet.

Anchor
Westminster Fibers
38 Westgate Crossing
Nashua, NH 03062
tel. 603 689 2448
info@westminsterfibers.com
www.westminsterfibers.com

Debbie Bliss
Knitting Fever Inc.
315 Bayview Avenue
Amityville, NY 11701
tel. + 1 516 546 3600
fax + 1 516 546 6871
www.knittingfever.com

DMC
The DMC Corporation
10 Basin Drive, Suite 130
Kearny, NJ 07032
tel. 973 589
fax 973 589 891
www.dmc-usa.com

Rowan
Westminster Fibers (as for Anchor)

Blogs and Websites I love:

www.etsy.com
(Lots of inspiration from other crocheters; good for yarn supplies too—hand spun or hand dyed.)

www.molliemakes.com
(Crochet tutorial and patterns. YouTube has some good tutorials.)

www.rosehip.typepad.com
(A lovely flower blanket crochet pattern I found here started me off on my floral phase.)

www.ilovepom-poms.squarespace.com
(Written by the awesome Cornel Strydom, based in South Africa, this blog curates the latest in crochet cool. Her Friday "craft share" images of the different girls at her craft circle, with their wonderful projects, are a must-see—I wish I could join them!)

www.creativemint.typepad.com
(Leslie is a seriously talented girl, living in Canada and bringing together inspirational color schemes. A lot of my crochet work starts with a color reference.)

www.emmallamb.blogspot.com
(Emma is another clever girl who loves her color. Her blog is awash with wonderful inspiration and lots of crochet, too—love it!)

www.craftstylish.com
(If you'd like to try making a Dorset button, you'll find step-by-step instructions here.)

… and so many more. Here are just a few that combine my love of crochet, stitching, and vintage in general:
- www.scrapiana.com
- www.inverleith.blogspot.com
- www.vintagemagpie.blogspot.com
- www.janeporcupine.blogspot.com
- www.attic24.typepad.com

Books I often refer to:

Handbook of Crochet Stitches: the Complete Illustrated Reference to Over 200 Stitches, by Betty Barnden (Search Press Ltd, 2009)

Around the Corner Crochet Borders, by Edie Eckman (Storey Publishing, 2010)

200 Crochet Blocks for Blankets, Throws and Afghans, by Jan Eaton (David & Charles, 2005)

Some shops I love:

Bead Shop, www.the-beadshop.co.uk +44 (0)845 2001818 (leather cord)

Dye for Yarn, www.etsy.com/shop/DyeForYarn (Nicole and Cordula in Nuremberg, suppliers of the gorgeous silk yarn used for the Lacy Scarf and Wrist Warmers.

Gemme Tresor, www.etsy.com/shop/GemmeTresor (Based in South Florida; gemstones and coral beads.)

Gone to Earth, www.gonetoearth.co.uk +44 (0)1933 623412 (Bamboo bag handles.)

Loop Knitting www.loopknitting.com (Suppliers of artisan yarn and indie patterns, they also offer a great range of courses.)

Purl Soho www.purlsoho.com (This New York store is a crafter's paradise. The website is full of beautiful images and luscious yarns)

Willow Fabrics, www.willowfabrics.com, +44 (0)1565 872225 (Online catalog of Anchor crochet cotton and linen threads; they also supply magnifiers—useful for fine work.)

Obviously, you will all have your own local yarn/fabric store, but I just want to say a big "thank you" to the ladies at the Wool & Craft Shop in Swanage, Dorset, to Jennifer at Thumbelina's in Wareham, Dorset and to all the girls at Daisy May's in Wareham (Fiona, Laura, Karen and Mary). I couldn't have done this book without all of your support, expertise and guidance.

ACKNOWLEDGMENTS

As is the case with most crafts, crochet brings people together. I have met some wonderful people along the way, and they have inspired and supported me throughout. First, though, a big "thank you" to my wonderful husband and children, who smile at my successes and giggle at the "Mummy, what is it?" experiments.

To my parents, who hold the fort when deadlines await. To Lena and all the ladies at the Wool Workshop, who offer advice and direction or just enthusiastic support. To Liz, for being my rock and ever-patient pattern tester. To my late grandmother, Connie, for starting me on my way all those years ago; I wish you could have seen this book.

To Laura and Fiona for patiently showing me how to sew. (It took me only five attempts to sew the zipper into the iPad case!)

To Alison, my publisher, who believed I could do this—I'm still not sure how I have done it, but your faith in me has played an enormous part in it. And to Clare, Eleanor, and Susan—editing a novice pattern writer's work is no easy task (wading through molasses springs to mind). Again, thank you all for your patience, guidance, and encouragement.

And finally, to Juliette and Anita for capturing my vision in their outstanding design, to Cynthia for her beautifully subtle styling, and Yuki for her sublime photography (not forgetting her lovely hardworking assistant, Kim). I am still a little overwhelmed that such talented, creative people agreed to work with my projects, so thank you for making them look so gorgeous.